REFLECTIONS

INSPIRATIONAL THOUGHTS

SELECTED BY CELEBRITIES

Researched and edited by Sue Gardner and Tony Noble.

Contributions also from the children, their families and friends of Sywell Church of England Voluntary Aided Primary School.

Jema Publications

First Published in 2012 by
Jema Publications

Copyright © Sue Gardner, Tony Noble 2012.

All rights reserved. No part of this publication
may be reproduced, stored in a retrieval system,
or transmitted in any form or by any means,
electronic, mechanical, photocopying, recording,
or otherwise, without the prior written permission
of the publishers.

This edition is published on behalf of the School Governors of
Sywell Church of England Voluntary Aided Primary School.

The Editors have asserted their right under the Copyright,
Designs and Patents Act 1988,
to be identified as the Editors of this Work.

ISBN: 9781871468540

Printed and bound in Great Britain by
Impress Print, Corby.

The Jema Publications website is
www.jemapublications.co.uk

Jema Publications
40 Ashley Lane
Moulton
Northampton   NN3 7TJ

CONTENTS

Contents	3
Acknowledgements	5
Introduction	6
Celebrities: Diamond Jubilee Prayer	7
His Holiness Pope Benedict XVI	8
Archbishop Vincent	9
Roger Royle	10
Joanna Lumley OBE	10
Lady Juliet Townsend	11
Bishop John of Brixworth	12
Frank Skinner	12
The Archbishop of York	13
Sir Alex Ferguson	13
John Griff	14
Bishop Donald Bishop of Peterborough	15
Bishop Wallace Bishop of Lewis	16/17
Susie Fowler-Watt	18
Johnnie Amos	19/20
Russell Grant	20
Alesha Dixon	21/22
Nigel Clough	23/24
Lord Sebastian Coe	25
Nigel Clough	25
Helen Skelton	26
Gyles Brandreth	26
Brian D'Arcy	27
Christine Ohuruogu MBE	28
Bishop of Northampton	29
Fern Britton	29
Sir Roger Bannister	30
Chris Heaton-Harris MP	31

Nick Clegg MP	32/33
David Capel	33
Aidy Boothroyd	34-38
Rick Wakeman	39
Revd Robert Mulford	40
Dame Judi Dench	41
Sally Magnussen	41
Graham Kendrick	42
Sir David Jason	43
Professor Andrew Wright	44
Gervase Phinn	45/46
Dr David Ison Dean of St Paul's	47
Nicholas Parsons OBE	48
Janey Lee Grace	49
Ken Dodd OBE	49
Paul Jones and Fiona Hendley Jones	50
Jimmy Cricket	50
Bobby Ball	51
Northleach CE Primary School	52
Bear Grylls	53
Dr Stephen Partridge	54
Rosemary Conley CBE & Mark Hanretty	55
Jimmy Tarbuck OBE	55
Lesley Pollard	56
Michael Morpurgo OBE	57
Fiona Castle OBE	58-60
Wendy Craig	61
Peter Goringe	62
Wendy Craig	62-64
Sir Tim Smit KBE	65-69
Michael Gove MP	70
Melanie Reid	71
Mike Ovey	72
Christine Burnett	73
Dorothy Carswell	73
Parents, Staff, Governors, Pupils and Friends	74
End Thoughts	124

> **Christian Education**
>
> **"Excelling in quality and distinctive in sharing God's love."**
>
> **Rt Revd Donald Allister
> Bishop of Peterborough**

ACKNOWLEDGEMENTS

Our thanks go to all who have contributed to this book, 60 celebrities and local personalities offering words of inspiration with a selection of 70 prayers and prose. Also to the parents, children, governors, staff and friends of Sywell Church of England Voluntary Aided Primary School who have offered prayers and prose to share. Without their contributions there would be no book.

Authors have been credited where known, but if we have omitted to credit any inclusions, or our efforts to make contact with copyright owners have been unsuccessful, please let us know and acknowledgements can be made in future editions.

Also thanks to the 'Sywell Old School Charity' and several donors for partly funding the cost of the production of the book.

INTRODUCTION

Our small church school of 100 children is located in the village of Sywell on the outskirts of Northampton. We are committed to providing a rich, inspiring and challenging curriculum for our children as well as an environment conducive to learning. To this end we have over the past few years, together with the Diocese of Peterborough raised funds to improve our class rooms and built a new and exciting 'green roofed' school hall. It is a facility we are proud of and often provides the 'wow' factor when seen for the first time.

This book is one of our innovative ways of helping to raise money. It is intended to provide inspiration and reflection through a collection of poems and prose, selected by celebrities, children, parents, staff, friends and governors.

We hope that you enjoy the contributions and that the words will provide you with some calmness in a busy world.
Thank you for your support.

Mrs Sue Gardner Headteacher
Dr John Herrick Chair of Governors

Prayer written at the Queen's request by the Chapter of St Paul's Cathedral for Her Majesty's Diamond Jubilee Year.

God of time and eternity,
whose Son reigns as servant, not master,
we give you thanks and praise
that you have blessed this Nation, the Realms and Territories
with ELIZABETH,
our beloved and glorious Queen.
In this year of Jubilee,
grant her your gifts of love and joy and peace
as she continues in faithful obedience to you, her Lord and God
and in devoted service to her lands and peoples,
and those of the Commonwealth,
now and all the days of her life;
through Jesus Christ our Lord.
Amen

A MESSAGE FROM HIS HOLINESS POPE BENEDICT XVI

SECRETARIAT OF STATE

FIRST SECTION - GENERAL AFFAIRS

From the Vatican, 11 October 2011

Dear Mr Noble,

The Holy Father has received your letter and he has asked me to send you this acknowledgment. He appreciates the sentiments which prompted you to write to him.

While it is not the practice for His Holiness to become directly involved in projects of the kind you mention, you may be assured of a remembrance in his prayers for your work in support of the education of the young people of your area.

With personal good wishes, I am

Yours sincerely,

Monsignor Peter B. Wells
Assessor

Lord,
bless all who feel strangers in your Church
and in our land.
Help us to open our hearts
to receive their gifts,
their experience,
their wisdom
which, in its truth,
is the fruit of your Holy Spirit.

Lord,
we thank you
for the richness of your Church,
and of our world.
Let no one be excluded
by our carelessness
and blindness.

Amen

Prayer written by
The Most Reverend Vincent Gerard Nichols
prior to becoming the
Eleventh Archbishop of Westminster
on
Thursday 21 May 2009

Archbishop Vincent is Head of the Roman Catholic Church.

Roger Royle, an Anglican Priest, author and broadcaster has chosen the following prayer. He has presented Sunday Half Hour on BBC 2, Songs of Praise, Pause for Thought with Terry Wogan on his weekday show and also a column for Woman's Weekly. He is also an author of several books.

"My favourite prayer is one that I think is particularly appropriate for a Primary School. It is the Breton Fisherman's prayer."

**Dear God, be good to me;
The sea is so wide
And my boat is so small.**
                                            Amen

Joanna Lumley is very fond of the following short prayer which was said by Sir Jacob Astley before the Battle of Newbury in September 1643:

"Lord I shall be verie busie this day. I may forget Thee: but doe not Thou forget me."

Joanna, an actress, former model and author is best known for her role in the British Television Series 'Absolutely Fabulous'. She has three BAFTA awards and a British Comedy Award.

~ 10 ~

Lady Juliet Townsend, Lord Lieutenant of Northamptonshire has chosen 'High Flight' written by John Magee during the Second World War and just before the young Canadian pilot was killed.

HIGH FLIGHT

Oh! I have slipped the surly bonds of earth,
And danced the skies on laughter-silvered wings;
Sunward I've climbed, and joined the tumbling mirth
Of sun-split clouds, and done a hundred things
You have not dreamed of - wheeled and soared and swung
High in the sunlit silence. Hov'ring there
I've chased the shouting wind along, and flung
My eager craft through footless hails of air
Up, up the long, delirious, burning blue
I've topped the wind-swept heights with easy grace
Where never lark or even eagle flew
And, while with silent lifting mind I've trod
The high untrespassed sanctity of space,
Put out my hand, and touched the face of God.

John Gillespie Magee, Jr.

'Face to Face'

Father God,
Bring us face to face with Jesus
And by your Holy Spirit
Make new Christians
And Christians new.
Amen

+John

'Face to Face' written for a mission in Bletchley and regularly used by The Rt Revd John Holbrook Bishop of Brixworth.

Dear Lord. When you were down here doing carpentry and stuff, did you know you were God? Did you always know? Did it dawn on you gradually? Did you have flashes of it and did you ever think, 'Whoah! I'm one of those mad blokes who thinks he's God.' You don't have to tell me. It's just that market-traders are all very hard and, when you overturned their stalls, I wondered if you had the old lightning-bolt up your sleeve. And if a very small human-being bit of you, which hadn't really mingled with your God-bit was thinking, 'Just you try it, Sunshine.'

Frank Skinner has chosen this prayer from his own autobiography. Frank a comedian, presenter, writer and actor is best known for his work in television. He is a practising Roman Catholic.

God, gather and turn my thoughts to you.
With you there is light, you do not forget me.
With you there is hope and patience.
I don't understand your ways, but you know the way for me.

+Sentrum

Words from The Archbishop of York that come from the Taize song, 'Aber du weilst den Weg fur mich' and adapted from a passage in Letters and Papers from Dietrich Bonhoeffer.

These words gave the Archbishop much comfort in a recent illness.

Sir Alex Ferguson CBE, Manager of Manchester United FC has chosen a verse from Ecclesiastes chapter 12 verse 2:

"Vanity of vanities, saith the preacher; all is vanity."

Death is nothing at all. I have only slipped away into the next room. I am I, and you are you. Whatever we were to each other, that we are still. Call me by my old familiar name, speak to me in the easy way which you always used. Put no differences in your tone, wear no forced air of solemnity or sorrow. Laugh as we have always laughed at the little jokes we enjoyed together. Play, smile, think of me, pray for me. Let my name be ever the household word that it always was. Let it be spoken without effect without the trace of a shadow on it. Life means all that it ever meant. It was the same as it ever was; there is unbroken continuity. What is this death but a negligible accident? Why should I be out of mind because I am out of sight? I am waiting for you, for an interval, somewhere very near, just around the corner. All is well.

**By Henry Scott Holland
1847-1918
Canon of St Paul's Cathedral**

John Griff says that 'Canon Henry Scott Holland's words proved to be of great comfort to me when a very close friend of mine lost his life. Death, is, for people of all ages a very difficult concept to come to terms with, but I think the Canon's words deal with it in a very constructive way by helping the reader to consider the unending spirit of the person who has died, rather than the fact of their death.'

Chosen by John Griff, Presenter of The Afternoon Programme, BBC Radio Northampton.

THE CREATION SONG FROM THE MAGICIAN'S NEPHEW BY C S LEWIS

If I find in myself desires nothing in this world can satisfy,
I can only conclude that I was not made for here.
If the flesh that I fight is at best only light and momentary,
Then of course I'll feel nude when to where I'm destined, I'm compared.

Speak to me in the light of the dawn
Mercy comes with the morning,
I will sigh and with all creation groan
As I wait for hope to come for me.

Am I lost or just less found on the straight or on the roundabout or the wrong way?
Is this a soul that stirs in me, is it breaking free, wanting to come alive?
'Cause my comfort would prefer for me to be numb
And avoid the impending birth of who I was born to become.

Speak to me in the light of the dawn
Mercy comes with the morning,
I will sigh and with all creation groan
As I wait for hope to come for me.

For we, we are not long here
Our time is but a breath, so we better breathe it
And I, I was made to live, I was made to love, I was made to know you.

Hope is coming for me
Hope is coming for me
Hope is coming for me
Hope is coming for me.

Speak to me in the light of the dawn
Mercy comes with the morning,
I will sigh and with all creation groan
As I wait for hope to come for me.
For me, for me, for me.

Chosen by Bishop Donald, Bishop of Peterborough

The Prayer of St Richard of Chichester

Thanks be to you, our Lord Jesus Christ,
for all the benefits which you have given us,
for all the pains and insults which you have borne for us.
Most merciful Redeemer, Friend and Brother,
may we know you more clearly,
love you more dearly,
and follow you more nearly,
day by day.

Amen

St Richard (1197-1253), who was Bishop of Chichester for eight years in the mid-13th century, was well acquainted with both hard work and suffering. Though a gifted scholar and lawyer, he did not flinch from physical labour; and as Bishop he found himself a homeless outcast in his own diocese, until King Henry III finally accepted his appointment by the Pope. His prayer reflects the commitment and 'stick ability' needed by anyone who seeks to be a true follower of Jesus.

Chosen by the Bishop of Lewis, the Rt Revd Wallace Benn.

Prayer of St Patrick

Christ be with me,
    Christ within me.
Christ behind me,
    Christ before me.
Christ beside me,
    Christ to win me.
Christ to comfort
    and restore me.
Christ beneath me,
    Christ above me.
Christ in quiet,
    Christ in danger.
Christ in hearts of
    All that love me.
CHRIST in mouth of
    friend and stranger.

Chosen by The Bishop of Lewis,
The Rt Revd Wallace Benn.

If a man does not keep pace with his companions, perhaps it is because he hears a different drummer. Let him step to the music which he hears, however measured or far away.

By Henry David Thoreau

Susie Fowler-Watt
Presenter
BBC Look East

There are many wonderful works of prose and prayers available to us and the theme of love flows throughout Christ's teaching.

Many waters cannot quench love,
neither can the floods drown it. Love is strong as death.
Greater love hath no man than this,
that a man lay down his life for his friends.
Who his own self bare our sins in his own body on the tree,
That we, being dead to sins, should live unto righteousness.
You are washed, you are sanctified,
you are justified in the name of the Lord Jesus.
You are a chosen generation, a royal priesthood, a holy nation;
That you should show forth the praises of him
who has called you out of darkness into his marvellous light.
I beseech you brothers and sisters, by the mercies of God,
that you present your bodies, a living sacrifice, holy acceptable to God, which is your reasonable service.

Words taken from the Songs of Soloman Ch 8 v 7 and the Gospel of John.

These words taken from both the Old and The New Testaments have remained with me all through my life and I have tried to live by them. Hope that this will be the same for the generations to come after me.

Johnnie Amos
BBC - Presenter and Producer
Horticulture

"My love of Shakespeare's numerous works say much about us in the past, present and future – but where to start, well Romeo and Juliet or Macbeth? The immortal words on Shakespeare's monument at Stratford-upon-Avon tell us why we should indulge ourselves in the Works of this genius."

Stay Passenger, why goest thou by so fast?
Read, if thou canst, whom envious death hath placed
Within this monument: Shakespeare, with whom
Quick nature died; whose name doth deck this tomb
Far more than cost, sith all that he hath writ
Leaves living art but page to serve his wit.

Johnnie Amos
BBC – Producer and Presenter
Horticulture

Russell Grant says, *"My favourite prayer is actually a very famous blessing taken from the Bible. It was written by St Francis to one of his earliest followers Brother Leo. Leo kept the Parchment on him for the rest of his life and it can now be found in the Basilica of St Francis in Assisi.*

Russell Grant is an astrologer who writes for a national paper and has taken part, very successfully, in Strictly Come Dancing.

"The Lord bless you and keep you.
May He show His face to you and have mercy.
May He turn His countenance to you and give you peace.
The Lord bless you!"

Alesha Dixon has chosen a favourite piece of prose written by Jasmine Richardson. Jasmine is the spiritual leader of a community of people, 'The Rose of Sharon Society.' This Society is a band of ordinary people' living ordinary lives, responding to a call to make prayer a priority.
Alesha is a singer, dancer, model and television presenter.

THE HIPPO'S TALE

As the wind of God's love
lifts me off my feet,
I see the beauty of yesteryear
far, far below,
but I also see the dazzling splendour
of where it is I am to go.

Up and up and up love lifts me,
to gaze upon the delicate grace
of a snowflake's face,
to marvel at the raindrop's gift of music,
to listen to the tale of the leaves,
rustling in the wind,
to bathe in the gentle beauty of the risen sun,
to walk along the footpaths of humility,
to dance in the magnificently jewelled
ballroom of obedience,
to rest so peacefully upon heaven's
featherbed of truth,
to sing a song of freedom from the tallest tree.

Gently does the wind of God's love
Put me down again,
With a silent whisper He commands:
"share what you have seen,"

Tentatively I knock at the door of
the hedgehog's abode:
alas his spines are in defensive mode –
he dare not look or listen.
Here comes the peacock.
Perhaps he will listen – too busy
is he with a proud display of his tail.

The snail surely will want to know –
but no – so paralysed with timidity
he runs into his shell.

To the ants I went next – will they
stop, look and listen?
Far too busy were they to think of Heaven.
Lord to whom shall I go?

"Have you met the starling with the broken wing,
the magpie with the one eye,
the toad with a growth on his head
or the spider who has lost a leg?"

Ah Lord, as a hippo with an aching heart,
here I can share the secrets of your love.

Susan J Richardson

"Dear Lord, in the struggle that goes on through life
We ask for a field that is fair,
A chance that is equal with all the strife,
The courage to strive and to dare;
And if we should win, let it be by the code,
With our faith and our honour held high;
And if we should lose, let us stand by the road
And cheer as the winners go by."

Prayer to Play Fair in the Game of Life – Knute Rockne
Nigel Clough thinks that this prayer is most appropriate for those involved with football.

Athlete's Prayer FISEC Games Malta 2008

"Help me play the game, dear Lord, with all my might and main;
Grant me the courage born of right, a heart to stand the strain...
Send me a sense of humour, Lord, to laugh when victory's mine,
When silence or some other thing wins plaudits from the throng...
When foes are tough and fighting fierce and I am getting weak,
Dear God, don't ever let me show a broad, bright, yellow streak.
And teach me, Lord, life's game to play just one day at a time.
With Thee as coach and trainer, Lord, real victory must be mine."

Chosen by Nigel Clough, former professional footballer who played more than 400 games for Nottingham Forest under the manager ship of his father Brian. Nigel also represented England and is now Manager of Derby County FC.

DEAR GOD, help me to be a good sport in life. I don't ask for an easy place in the line-up.
Put me anywhere you need me. I only ask that I can give you 100% of everything I have. If all the hard tackles seem to come my way, I thank you for the compliment. Help me to remember that you never send a player more trouble than he can handle with your help…
And help me, Lord, to accept the bad breaks as part of the game. May I always play on the pitch no matter what others do… Help me study… THE BOOK so I'll know the rules…
Finally, God, if the natural turn of events goes against me and I am benched for sickness or old age, help me accept that as part of the game, too. Keep me from whimpering that I was framed or that I got a raw deal. And when I finish the final match, I ask for no laurels; all I want is to believe in my heart, I played as well as I could and that I didn't let you down. Amen.

Cardinal Richard Cushing

Chosen by Nigel Clough the Manager of Derby County Football Club and former professional with Nottingham Forest and England.

Sebastian Coe Chairman of The London Organising Committee of the Olympic Games and Paralympic Games Ltd, has chosen these words from Robert F Kennedy.

"Only those who dare to fail greatly can ever achieve greatly."

Robert F Kennedy, Day of Affirmation speech at the University of Cape Town, 6 June 1966.

Sebastian Coe was a 1500 metres gold medal winner at the 1980 and 1984 Olympic Games.

Do you not know that runners in the stadium all run in the race, but only one wins the prize? Run so as to win. Every athlete exercises discipline in every way. They do it to win a perishable crown, but we an imperishable one. Thus I do not run aimlessly, I do not fight as if I were shadowboxing.
No I drive my body and train it, for fear that, after having preached to others, I myself should be disqualified.
1 Corinthians Chapter 9 verses 24 to 27

Chosen by Nigel Clough, Manager of Derby County Football Club and former professional with Nottingham Forest and England.

Helen Skelton of Blue Peter has a framed wall hanging that says:

**Dance as if no one is looking
Sing as if no one can hear
Laugh as if no one is listening ……..**

….. I also believe that you get out of life what you put in.

Helen Skelton Blue Peter, with best wishes from Helen, Barney and all at Blue Peter.

Gyles Brandreth has chosen, 'a nice thought from Hilaire Belloc'.

**'From quiet homes and first beginning
Out to the undiscovered ends
There's nothing worth the wear of winning
But laughter and the love of friends.'**

Giles is an author, broadcaster, actor and entertainer. Perhaps more recently known for his appearances on the BBC 1 One Show.

Where Am I Going?

My Lord God, I have no idea where I am going,
I do not see the road ahead of me.
I cannot know for certain where it will end.
Nor do I really know myself, and the fact that I think I am following Your will does not mean that I am actually doing so.
But I believe that the desire to please You does in fact please You.
And I hope that I have that desire in all that I am doing.
I hope that I will never do anything apart from that desire.
And I know that if I do this, You will lead me by the right road.
Though I may know nothing about it.
Therefore I will trust you always though
I may seem to be lost and in the shadow of death.
I will not fear, for You are ever with me,
And You will never leave me to face my perils alone.

This was Brian D'Arcy's choice, the 'Prayer by Thomas Merton, cited in "A Different Journey" by Brian D'Arcy.

Brian D'Arcy is one of Ireland's best known priests. He is an accomplished author, broadcaster, journalist and chaplain to the entertainment industry.

Take Time chosen by Christine Ohuruogu the Beijing Olympic 400 metre Champion. Christine was also 400 metre champion at the 2006 Commonwealth Games and the 2007 World Championships. Christine came second in the London Olympics 2012 winning the silver medal.

Take Time
Take time to think – it is the source of power.
Take time to read – it is the foundation of wisdom.
Take time to play – it is the secret of staying young.
Take time to be quiet – it is the opportunity to seek God.
Take time to be aware – it is the opportunity to help others.
Take time to love – it is God's greatest gift.
Take time to laugh – it is the music of the soul.
Take time to be friendly – it is the road to happiness.
Take time to dream – it is what the future is made of.
Take time to pray – it is the greatest power on earth.
There is a time for everything ……

Today, take time, or rather make time for what's really important in your life. Remember to share a smile, give a hug, hold the door open for another person, be courteous when driving, call someone you haven't talked to for a while. Life is too short to go around living it with anger or hatred.

The Roman Catholic Bishop of Northampton
The Rt Revd Peter Doyle has chosen a favourite
prayer from the conclusion to Morning Prayer.

**Lord, be the beginning and end
of all that we do and say.
Prompt our actions with your grace,
and complete them with your all-powerful help.
This we ask through Christ our Lord. Amen.**

Fern Britton chooses this prayer which was given to her during a difficult time.

Fern says, "I say this to myself when I am scared or unhappy and it gives me strength. I hope the children like it too!"

**Jesus Christ is with me, and all is well.
Amen
(Anon)**

Fern Britton, television presenter is possibly best known as the former co-presenter of ITV's 'This Morning'.

~ 29 ~

Christmas Bells

I HEARD the bells on Christmas Day
Their old, familiar carols play,
   And wild and sweet
   The words repeat
Of peace on earth, good-will to men!

And thought how, as the day had come,
The belfries of all Christendom
   Had rolled along
   The unbroken song
Of peace on earth, good-will to men!

Till ringing, singing on its way,
The world revolved from night to day,
   A voice, a chime,
   A chant sublime
Of peace on earth, good-will to men!

Then from each black, accursed mouth
The cannon thundered in the South,
   And with the sound
   The carols drowned
Of peace on earth, good-will to men!

It was as if an earthquake rent
The hearth-stones of a continent,
   And made forlorn
   The households born
Of peace on earth, good-will to men!

And in despair I bowed my head;
"There is no peace on earth," I said;
   "For hate is strong,
   And mocks the song
Of peace on earth, good-will to men!"

Then pealed the bells more loud and deep:
"God is not dead, nor doth He sleep;
   The Wrong shall fail,
   The Right prevail,
With peace on earth, good-will to men."

Sir Roger Bannister has chosen this seasonal poem by Henry W Longfellow. Sir Roger was the first athlete to run the mile in under 4 minutes. This achievement on 6th May 1954 at Oxford set a new world record of 3 minutes 59 seconds.

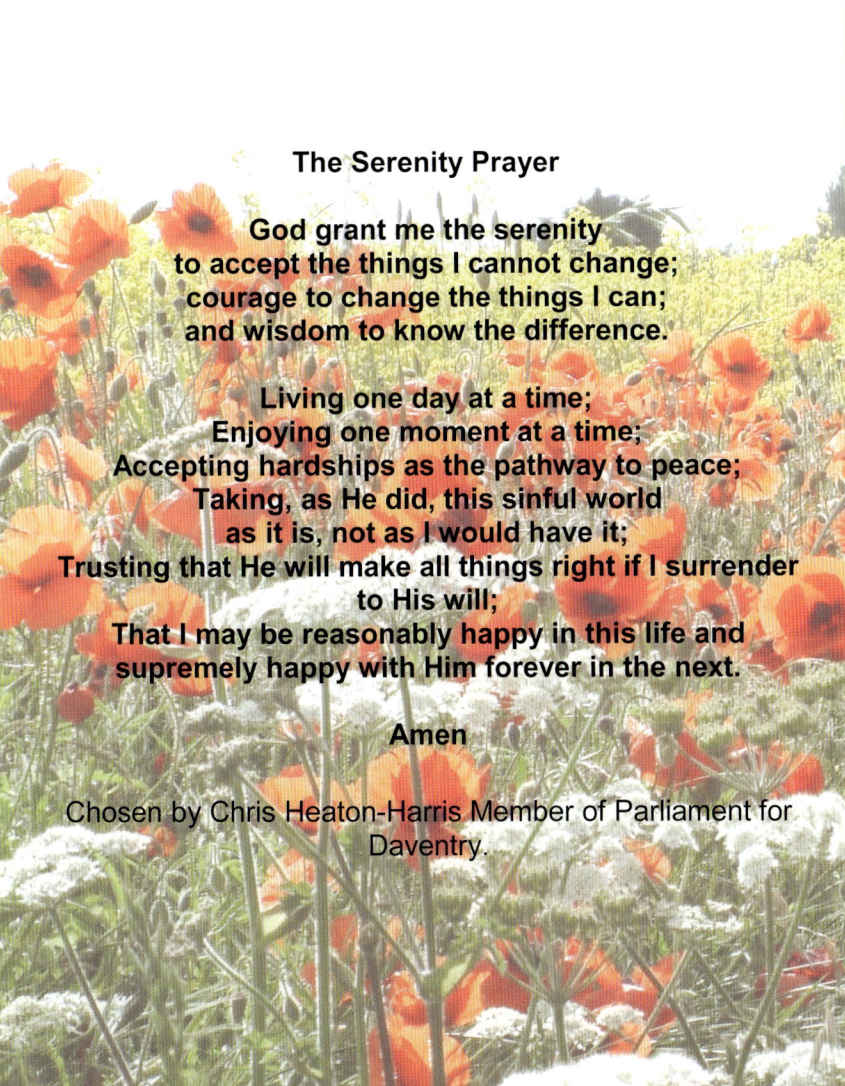

The Serenity Prayer

God grant me the serenity
to accept the things I cannot change;
courage to change the things I can;
and wisdom to know the difference.

Living one day at a time;
Enjoying one moment at a time;
Accepting hardships as the pathway to peace;
Taking, as He did, this sinful world
as it is, not as I would have it;
Trusting that He will make all things right if I surrender
to His will;
That I may be reasonably happy in this life and
supremely happy with Him forever in the next.

Amen

Chosen by Chris Heaton-Harris Member of Parliament for Daventry.

Nick Clegg Member of Parliament, Liberal Democrat leader and Deputy Prime Minister has this very famous prose by Rudyard Kipling hanging prominently in his Westminster Office and sent this offering.

IF

If you can keep your head when all about you
Are losing theirs and blaming it on you;
If you can trust yourself when all men doubt you,
But make allowance for their doubting too;
If you can wait and not be tired of waiting.
Or being lied about, don't deal in lies,
Or being hated don't give way to hating,
And yet don't look too good, nor talk too wise.

If you can dream – and not make dreams your master.
If you can think – and not make thoughts your aim.
If you can meet with Triumph and Disaster.
And treat those two impostors just the same;
If you can bear to hear the truth you've spoken
Twisted by knaves to make a trap for fools,
Or watch the things you gave your life to broken,
And stoop and build 'em up with worn out tools.

If you can make one heap of all your winnings
And risk it on one turn of pitch-and-toss,
And lose, and start again at your beginnings
And never breathe a word about your loss;
If you can force your heart and nerve and sinew
To serve your turn long after they are gone,
And so hold on when there is nothing in you
Except the Will which says to them "Hold on!"

If you can talk with crowds and keep your virtue,
Or walk with Kings – nor lose the common touch,
If neither foes nor loving friends can hurt you,
If all men count with you, but none too much;
If you can fill the unforgiving minute,
With sixty seconds worth of distance run,
Yours is the earth and everything that's in it,
And – which is more – you'll be a Man, my son!

By Rudyard Kipling

A PRAYER OF HOPE, FAITH AND THANKSGIVING.

Dear Lord

Thanks for the guidance of my teachers, family and friends
Help them to have patience, courage and strength
Always kind, forgiving, peaceful and happy
Never let them lose hope or faith
Keep them content and safe
Show them wisdom from above, your generosity and lots of love.

Lord hear my prayer.

Amen

Written by David Capel, former Head Coach and 1st Team Manager at Northants Cricket. David Capel, an all-rounder played professional cricket for Northamptonshire between 1981 and 1998, and represented England in 15 test matches and 23 One Day Internationals.

The Race chosen by Aidy Boothroyd Manager of Northampton Town Football Club who says, "Whilst I appreciate this is rather long I find the message throughout to be extremely motivational."

THE RACE
by Dee Groberg

"Quit! Give up! You're beaten!"
They shout at me, and plead
"There's just too much against you now.
This time you can't succeed."

And as I start to hang my head
In front of failure's face
My downward fall is broken by
The memory of a race.

And hope refills my weakened will
As I recall that scene
For, just the thought of that short race
Rejuvenates my being.

A children's race, young boys, young men
Now, I remember well,
Excitement, sure! But also fear,
It wasn't hard to tell.

They all lined up so full of hope
Each thought to win that race,
Or, tie for first, if not that,
At least take second place.

And fathers watched from off the side
Each cheering for his son.
And each boy hoped to show his dad,
That he would be the one.

The whistle blew, and off they went.
Young hearts and hopes afire
To win, to be the hero there
Was each young boy's desire.

And one boy in particular,
Whose dad was in the crowd,
Was running near the head and thought
"My dad will be so proud!"

But as they speeded down the field
Across a shallow dip
The little boy who thought to win,
Lost his step and slipped

Trying hard to catch himself,
His hands flew out to brace
And 'mid the laughter of the crowd
He fell flat on his face.

So, down he fell, and with him hope
- he couldn't win it now -
Embarrassed, sad, he only wished
To disappear somehow.

But, as he fell, his dad stood up,
And showed his anxious face,
Which to the boy so clearly said:
"Get up and win the race."

He quickly rose, no damage done,
- behind a bit, that's all -
And ran with all his mind and might
To make up for his fall.

So, anxious to restore himself
- to catch up and to win -
His mind went faster than his legs;
He slipped and fell again!

He wished, then, he had quit before
With only one disgrace.
"I'm hopeless as a runner now;
I shouldn't try to race.

But, in the laughing crowd he searched
And found his father's face.
That steady look that said again!
"Get up and win the race."

So, up he jumped, to try again
- ten yards behind the last -
"If I'm to gain those yards," he thought
"I've got to move real fast."

Exceeding everything he had
He gained back eight or ten,
But trying so, to catch the lead,
He slipped and fell again.

Defeat! He lay there silently
- a tear dropped from his eye -
"There is no sense in running more;
Three strikes, I'm out, why try?"

The will to rise had disappeared
All hope had fled away
So far behind; so error prone
A loser all the way.

"I've lost, so what's the use," he thought
"I'll live with my disgrace."
But, then he thought about his dad,
Who, soon, he'd have to face.

"Get up!" an echo sounded low,
"Get up, and take your place
You were not meant for failure here,
Get up, and win the race."

With borrowed will, "Get up," it said
"You haven't lost at all.
For winning is no more than this;
To rise each time you fall."

So, up he rose to run once more,
And with a new commit
He resolved that win, or lose,
At least he wouldn't quit.

So far behind the others now
- the most he'd ever been -
Still, he gave it all he had,
And ran as though to win.

Three times he'd fallen stumbling.
Three times he'd rose again.
Too far behind to hope to win
He still ran to the end.

They cheered the winning runner,
As he crossed the line first place,
Head high, and proud, and happy
No falling, no disgrace.

But, when the fallen youngster
Crossed the line last place,
The crowd gave him the greater cheer
For finishing the race.

Even though he came in last.
With head bowed head low, unproud,
You would have thought he won the race
To listen to the crowd.

And to his dad, he sadly said,
"I didn't do so well."
"To me, you won!" his father said,
"You rose each time you fell."

And now when things seem dark and hard,
And difficult to face.
The memory of that little boy
Helps me to win my race.

For all of life is like that race
With ups and downs and all,
And all you have to do to win,
Is rise each time you fall.

This prayer was chosen by Rick Wakeman, it is in his book 'SAY YES' and permanently on his website. Rick says, "I think it says everything. It is a prayer attributed to an unknown confederate soldier, whom I consider a kindred spirit."

I asked for strength that I might achieve;
I was made weak that I may learn humbly to obey.
I asked for health that I might do greater things;
I was given infirmity that I might do better things.
I asked for riches that I might be happy;
I was given poverty that I might be wise.
I asked for power that I might have the praise of men;
I was given weakness that I might feel the need of God.
I asked for all things that I might enjoy life;
I was given life that I might enjoy all things.
I got nothing that I had asked for;
But everything I had hoped for.
Almost despite myself my unspoken prayers were answered;
I am, among all men, most richly blessed.

Rick Wakeman is a Baptist who is famous all around the world for his music and compositions.

FREE GIFT

You have been selected for a free gift

No, it isn't double glazing

Or a time share, or a kitchen

But someone is in your area

It's free, no cost, no worry

You don't even have to leave your home

You don't have to move

It will be with you where ever you go

Interested?

Peace be with you.

Rev Robert Mulford, former curate at Great Billing and having worked with the children at St Paul and St Nicholas Churches, Sywell and Overstone is now the vicar of two parishes in Guestling near Hastings.
This was written in 1995 as part of a series of poems for a London Radio, whilst working as a Headteacher in the capital.

Dame Judi Dench, actress starring in television, stage, and film has chosen this by Francis Thompson and William Blake as one of her favourites.

Know you what it is to be a child? ... It is to have a spirit yet streaming from the waters of baptism; it is to believe in love, to believe in loveliness, to believe in belief; it is to be so little that the elves can reach to whisper in your ear; it is to turn pumpkins into coaches, and mice into horses, lowness into loftiness, and nothing into everything – for each child has a fairy god-mother in his/her own soul; it is to live in a nutshell and count yourself the king/queen of infinite space; it is:
To see the World in a grain of sand,
And a heaven in a wild flower,
Hold infinity in the palm of your hand,
And eternity in an hour.

Chosen by Sally Magnussen, a TV presenter including Songs of Praise, and as she says, "The words may be old fashioned, but this blessing – often sung in Scottish churches after the baptism of an infant – is for everyone, young and old.
A blessing for life."

The Lord bless thee and keep thee.
The Lord make his face to shine upon thee
And be gracious unto thee.
The Lord lift up his countenance upon thee
And give thee peace.
Amen

(Numbers 6, 24-26)

Graham Kendrick a well-known evangelist and writer of Christian songs and plays offers this prayer in which he says, "Some prayers are written to be sung, and this is one of those. It was a time in my life when things were not working out as I had hoped, and although I had already decided to follow Jesus, and trust my future to God, I was trying to work it all out myself, and as a result getting anxious and impatient. This was my prayer of commitment to deeper trust."

In Your way and in Your time
That's how it's going to be
In my life

And in Your perfect way I'll rest my weary mind
And as You lead I'll follow close behind
And in Your presence I will know Your peace is mine
In Your time there is rest
There is rest

In Your way and in Your time
That's how it's going to be
In my life

Dear Jesus soothe me now till all my strivings cease
Kiss me with the beauty of Your peace
And I will wait and not be anxious at the time
In Your time there is rest
There is rest

And though some prayers I've prayed may seem unanswered yet
You never come too quickly or too late
And I will wait and I will not regret the time
In Your time there is rest
There is rest

Graham Kendrick ©1976 Make Way Music.
www.grahamkendrick.co.uk

Sir David Jason offers Rev Eli Jenkins' Prayer from 'Under Milk Wood' by Dylan Thomas.

Every morning when I wake,
Dear Lord, a little prayer I make,
O please do keep Thy lovely eye
On all poor creatures born to die.

And every evening at sun-down
I ask a blessing on the town,
For whether we last the night or no
I'm sure is always touch-and-go.

We are not wholly bad or good
Who live our lives under Milk Wood,
And Thou, I know, wilt be the first
To see our best side, not our worst.

O let us see another day!
Bless us all this night, I pray,
And to the sun we all will bow
And say, good-bye – but just for now!

Sir David Jason, actor, is best known for his character of Derek 'Del Boy' Trotter in the BBC sitcom 'Only Fools and Horses'. David has made many television appearances in a variety of dramas including 'The Darling Buds of May'.

Andrew Wright Professor of Religious and Theological Education at King's College London chooses the hymn: 'Now Thank We All Our God', a translation of Martin Rinkart's 'Nun danket alle Gott' (c.1636). It combines the simplicity of the Christian Gospel with the profundity of Trinitarian doctrine, and was, incidentally, also the favourite hymn of one of the greatest Christian theologians of the modern age, Karl Barth.

**Now thank we all our God, with heart and hands and voices,
Who wondrous things has done, in Whom this world rejoices;
Who from our mother's arms has blessèd us on our way
With countless gifts of love, and still is ours today.**

**O may this bounteous God through all our life be near us,
With ever joyful hearts and blessed peace to cheer us;
And keep us in His grace, and guide us when perplexed;
And free us from all ills, in this world and the next!**

**All praise and thanks to God the Father now be given;
The Son and Him Who reigns with Them in highest Heaven;
The one eternal God, whom earth and Heaven adore;
For thus it was, is now, and shall be evermore.**

Gervase Phinn is a teacher, freelance lecturer, author, poet, school inspector and educational consultant. He is probably best known for his books and writings on school life in the Yorkshire Dales and more recently his one man shows in theatres around the country. Truly a great raconteur.

Gervase has chosen two of his own poems which are most appropriate for this anthology and give very important and poignant messages.

A Message for Mums and Dads

(Acrostic)

Teach me compassion.
Help to keep an open mind and respect the views of others.
Expect a lot of me.

Allow me some space.
Don't tell me my dreams are wild and my fears are foolish.
Offer advice now and again, but please don't nag.
Listen to what I have to say.
Encourage me and please don't criticise me in front of others.
Support me and realise that – once in a while – I can be difficult.
Cope with my moods and try to be a bit more patient.
Enjoy my successes but please don't be disappointed in my shortcomings.
Never make promises you can never keep.
Take no notice when I say hurtful things, I don't mean them.

A Father's ABC of Life

(Alphabet poem)

Always remember my son to:

Act in a manner that you would wish to be treated,
Be considerate and show compassion,
Choose your friends with care,
Don't take yourself too seriously,
Enjoy all that life offers you,
Follow your dreams,
Guard against bitterness and envy,
Harm no one,
Ignore the cynic,
Jog a little each day,
Keep calm in a crisis,
Laugh a lot,
Make the best of what you have got,
Never miss an opportunity of saying "Thank You",
Open your heart to those you love,
Pay no attention to grumblers,
Question certainties,
Respect the feelings of others,
Stay true to your principles,
Take a few measured risks,
Use your talents wisely,
Value your family,
Work hard,
X-pect a lot of yourself – but not too much,
Yearn not for riches,
Zest for living should be your aim in this world.

Gervase Phinn

The Very Reverend Dr David Ison Dean of St Paul's Cathedral, London has chosen "The Bright Field" by RS Thomas. The Dean says; "I've loved this poem since I discovered it years ago. It's become a reminder of why I have been and remain a follower of Jesus Christ, ever since I went looking in the world for goodness and beauty that would last."

The poem refers to two stories in the Bible. Jesus told the story of a man who found a pearl of great price in a field, and sold everything so that he could buy the field and own the pearl. And Moses had the courage to turn aside from everyday things to find God in something unusual and unexpected, a bush which was burning in the wilderness. R.S.Thomas reminds us to keep our sense of wonder, always: not to be too busy or distracted to look for light and treasure, and to follow our hearts in order to find God.

> I have seen the sun break through
> to illuminate a small field
> for a while, and gone my way
> and forgotten it. But that was the pearl
> of great price, the one field that had
> treasure in it. I realize now
> that I must give all that I have
> to possess it. Life is not hurrying
> on to a receding future, nor hankering after
> an imagined past. It is turning
> aside like Moses to the miracle
> of the lit bush, to a brightness
> that seemed as transitory as your youth
> once, but is the eternity that awaits you.

Nicholas Parsons the actor, broadcaster and presenter chooses a section from The Prophet by Kahlil Gibran. The Prophet is writing for the children.

CHILDREN

Your children are not your children.
They are the sons and daughters of Life's longing for itself.
They come through you but not from you,
And though they are with you, yet they belong not to you.
You may give them your love but not your thoughts.
For they have their own thoughts.
You may house their bodies but not their souls,
For their souls dwell in the house of tomorrow, which you cannot visit, not even in your dreams.
You may strive to be like them, but seek not to make them like you.
For life goes not backward nor tarries with yesterday.
You are the bows from which your children as living arrows are sent forth.
The archer sees the mark upon the path of the infinite, and He bends you with His might that His arrows may go swift and far.
Let your bending in the archer's hand be for gladness;
For even as he loves the arrow that flies, so He loves also the bow that is stable.

Janey Lee Grace is best known as Steve Wright's co-presenter on the popular afternoon show on Radio 2. Janey Lee has great belief in the power of prayer.

*Dear God,
You know my need; please help (as if you wouldn't; as if you haven't already); bring relief to searching; bring an end to striving; bring peace and stillness and new life. Christ, put my feet on the right path.
Amen.

*Clown's Prayer chosen by Ken Dodd

As I stumble through this life, help me to create more laughter than tears, dispense more happiness than gloom, spread more cheer than despair.

Never let me become so indifferent that I will fail to see the wonder in the eyes of a child or the twinkle in the eyes of the aged.

Never let me forget that my total effort is to cheer people, make them happy and forget – at least momentarily – all the unpleasantness in their lives.

And, in my final moment, may I hear You whisper; 'When you made My people smile, you made Me smile'.

Author unknown

Ken Dodd and his Diddymen from Knotty Ash are household names and are wrapped up in Ken's comedy act.

*'Reaching for the Stars' – The Entertainers Prayerbook – Chris Gidney – published by Canterbury Press. WWW.cieweb.org.uk

Paul Jones and Fiona Hendley Jones offer this prayer they have written for all Christians in Entertainment – a prayer to use talents wisely. Paul was lead singer in the 1960's with the Manfred Mann group and was perhaps best known for the song 'Pretty Flamingo'. He continues with his singing but is also an actor. Fiona is also a singer and actress. They met whilst seeking their Christian faith.

*Father, Thank you that, through your Son Jesus, I am now aware just how much you love me; You also gave me talent, a gift to perform. O Lord, put your hand upon all Christians in Entertainment at this time. Give us the strength to use that gift to the very best of our ability, and help us to reflect your truth to all those with whom we are working. May we glorify your holy name in excellence and love, for the sake of your Son, who died for us, and rose again to bring us new life. Amen

Jimmy Cricket is a comedian famous for his catchphrase, 'And there's more'. He was brought up in Ireland where he went to church regularly on Sunday and it was here that his faith developed. Jimmy's own prayer is for strength.

*Prayer for Strength

Heavenly Father, help me to relax when times are hard, and know that there's a higher power guiding me. Give me the serenity to smile through the lean times, give me the faith and confidence to know that if I do my best for you, everything else will be taken care of. And most of all, help me to use the talent you have given me to enrich people's lives with love and laughter.
Through your son, Jesus Christ. Amen

*'Reaching for the Stars' – The Entertainers Prayerbook – Chris Gidney – published by Canterbury Press. WWW.cieweb.org.uk

Bobby Ball likes writing poems and this prayer is the closing section of one poem he has written. Bobby is part of the Cannon and Ball comedy act and his partner Tommy Cannon also has a strong faith.

*Power of Prayer

Please forgive me, but I find it hard to apologise,
To be able to see the other person's point of view.
But deep inside, behind all this sinful pride,
I want to be just like you.

Really deep in my soul, I want to be sensitive,
I want to open my eyes and see.
I no longer want this pride to be ever consuming,
I want to trade for humility.

As Jesus said, pride is a sin
And it will eventually bring about a man's fall.
You See, I've been too busy being proud
I didn't listen to Jesus' call.

If only you could forgive me, Jesus,
For my sins, but most of all my pride.
Forgive, for all the people my pride hurt,
And for the way to myself I lied.

So fill me, Jesus with your love,
Fill me to my innermost being.
Take away this mask from my eyes,
Give me joy like a blind man first upon seeing.

Earnestly I beg you Jesus,
Wash away my sin as only you can,
And turn this arrogant and ignorant thing
Into a brand new humble man.

*'Reaching for the Stars' – The Entertainers Prayerbook – Chris Gidney – published by Canterbury Press. WWW.cieweb.org.uk

What is God is a poem written by 7 and 8 year olds in Class 3 at Northleach CE Primary School.

What is God?

**God is not against you
God is not young
God is not a man
God is not human
God is not weak
God is not a slave
God is not an enemy
God is not evil
God is not a sun
God is not a cloud
God is not on earth
God is not on the earth with you
God is not killing the earth
God is not solid
God is not in sight
God is not unfriendly
God is not lonely
God is not different
God is not disappointed.**

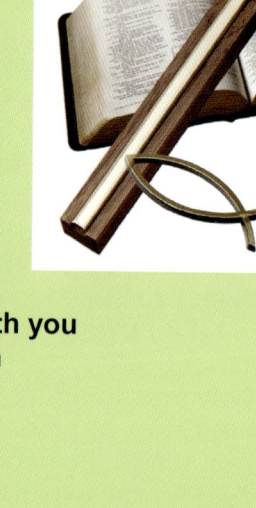

© Class 3, Northleach CE Primary School, Mill End, Northleach GL54 3HJ and RE Today Services. Source: from Retoday, vol 29, no 2, Autumn 2011.

For those of us who spend a lot time away from our families, whether as serving soldiers or just away from work, we focus a lot on the magic of 'coming' home. But life is also about 'finding' our home.

Let me explain.

You see, faith is sometimes hard to talk openly about; and faith, if it is to be real and meaningful, is of course intensely personal. But that is also part of what makes believing so special.

I have learnt though, over the years, from numerous expeditions, close calls and hairy moments, from Everest, through to my time in the SAS, the Arctic and the Antarctic, that it takes a proud man to say that he never needs help. And I have yet to meet an atheist in Everest's Death Zone or in a lifeboat!

Life is a journey and we all, at times, need a guide. But that Guide, for me, has become much more than simply a pointer of the way. He has become my backbone, my confidante, my helper, my companion and my friend.

If we look back in time, there are not many great men, women or leaders who have not, quietly in their hearts, bent the knee and looked upwards to Jesus for help, strength, resolve and peace in the big moments.

Look at the lives of people like Isaac Newton or the Wright brothers or Joan of Arc and Abraham Lincoln. Nelson Mandela, Galileo, and of course the Scouting founder, Baden-Powell, to name but a few. All were men or women of great influence. All were men or women of faith.

Indeed it takes a proud man to say he never needs help.

It has taken me some time, and whole hosts of getting it wrong, finally to have the courage to bend that knee and admit a quiet need for my Christian faith – but what a world, what comfort, what a revelation, it has been since.

That's what I mean by coming home.
Bear Grylls
Chief Scout

*Dear Lord, in my busy day-to-day life, while I am focused on my priorities, help me to be aware of all those around me, let me hear when others are distressed and need comforting, give me the insight to see where others are hurting, support me in reaching out to others who resist my help, and give me the grace to allow others to help me.
Amen*

Stephen Partridge
Diocesan Director of Education, Peterborough Diocese (1999-2012).

Sarah

Lord, thank you for this body that you have given to me to use during my life time. Please help me to nourish it well so that I may grow and be healthy. Help me to be energetic enough to keep my body fit and working efficiently so that I may achieve my dreams. Lord, help me to be kind and caring to others and to forgive those who are mean to me. Thank you for loving me always. Amen

*By Rosemary Conley CBE, Diet and Fitness Expert
Mark Hanretty, International Professional Ice Skater.*

Rosemary Conley and Mark Hanretty competed in ITV's Dancing on Ice 2012.

Jimmy Tarbuck OBE has this as his favourite text of all time.
Jimmy Tarbuck, a comedian who has hosted many quiz and variety shows including from 1965 the famous 'Sunday Night at the London Palladium'. He supports Liverpool FC, the city where he was born. A keen golfer and supporter of charity events.

**This life I have is all I have
This life I have is yours
But the love I have for this life I have is
yours and yours and yours.**

Lesley Pollard, School Improvement Officer in Northamptonshire has chosen a poem that has inspired her throughout her teaching.
William Crockett's poem sums up what school should be about – a place to cry, fly, seek, speak, learn and be oneself. I always tried to ensure my classroom was such a place and hope that it proved to be so for children and young people who spent time there.

A People Place

If this is not a place where tears are understood,
Where do I go to cry?
If this is not a place where my spirits can take wing,
Where do I go to fly?
If this is not a place where my questions can be asked,
Where do I go to seek?
If this is not a place where my feelings can be heard,
Where do I go to speak?
If this is not a place where you'll accept me as I am,
Where can I go to be?
If this is not a place where I can try to learn and grow,
Where can I be just me?

Michael Morpurgo, former Children's Laureate is one of the most popular authors writing for children. Michael is a natural storyteller and is probably best known for his highly successful book 'War Horse'. Michael's choice is 'The Lamb' by William Blake.

The Lamb

    Little Lamb, who made thee?
    Dost thou know who made thee?
Gave thee life, and bid thee feed
By the stream and o'er the mead;
Gave thee clothing of delight,
Softest clothing, woolly bright;
Gave thee such a tender voice,
Making all the vales rejoice?
    Little Lamb, who made thee?
    Dost thou know who made thee?

    Little Lamb, I'll tell thee,
    Little Lamb, I'll tell thee:
He is called by thy name,
For he calls himself a Lamb.
He is meek, and he is mild;
He became a little child.
I a child and thou a lamb.
We are called by his name.
    Little Lamb, God bless thee!
    Little Lamb, God bless thee!

The Lamb was first published in 1785. Like many of Blake's works the poem is about Christianity.

Fiona Castle OBE chose this prayer by AW Tozer which she says, "is such a challenge to me. When I became a Christian at the age of 35 I invited Jesus into my life, recognising that I had made a mess of my life up to that time, by trying to run it my way, and asking Him to do what He wanted with the rest of it. I really meant it and I still do mean it, but this prayer makes me realise how meagre my offering very often is."

I come to you today, O Lord,
To give up my rights,
To lay down my life,
To offer my future,
To give my devotion, my skills, my energies.
I shall not waste time
Deploring my weaknesses
Nor my unfittedness for the work.
I acknowledge your choice with my life
To make your Christ attractive and intelligible
To those around me.
I come to you for spiritual preparation.
Put your hand on me,
Anoint me with the oil of the one with Good News.
Save me from compromise,
Heal my soul from small ambitions,
Deliver me from the itch always to be right,
Save me from wasting time.
I accept hard work, I ask for no easy place,
Help me not to judge others who walk a smoother path.
Show me those things that diminish spiritual power in a soul.
I now consecrate my days to you.
Make your will more precious than anybody or anything.
Fill me with your power
And when at the end of life's journey I see you face to face
May I hear those undeserving words,
"Well done, you good and faithful servant."
I ask this not for myself,
But for the glory of your Son.

Fiona Castle OBE, best known for her marriage to the late entertainer Roy Castle. Since her husband's death she has continued her charity work.

BLESSED BE YOUR NAME

Blessed be your name
In the land that is plentiful,
Where your streams of abundance flow,
Blessed be your name.

Blessed be your name,
When I'm found in the desert place,
Though I walk through the wilderness,
Blessed be your name.

Every blessing you pour out
I'll turn back to praise
And when the darkness closes in Lord
Still I will say,
Blessed be the name of the Lord
Blessed be your name.
Blessed be the name of the Lord
Blessed be your glorious name.

Blessed be your name
When the sun's shining down on me,
When the world's all that it should be,
Blessed be your name.

Blessed be your name,
On the road marked with suffering,
Though there's pain in the offering,
Blessed be your name.

Every blessing you pour out
I'll turn back to praise
And when the darkness closes in Lord
Still I will say,
Blessed be the name of the Lord
Blessed be your name.
Blessed be the name of the Lord
Blessed be your glorious name.

You give and take away,
You give and take away,
My heart will choose to say,
Lord blessed be your name.

Matt Redman

Fiona Castle imagines this wonderful song of Matt Redman's was inspired by the verses from the book of Job.
Chapter 1 v 21, "The Lord gives, and the Lord takes away. Blessed be the name of the Lord."
This verse meant so much to me many years ago, when my son nearly died after a fall. As I was helping the medical staff wheel him into the intensive care ward, the only thing I could think of were these words. I repeated them again and again, knowing that God was in control and that we were safe in His hands. It is easy to praise God when things are going well, but it is challenging to praise Him in the tough times!
"In everything give thanks." Ephesians chapter 5 v 20.

Wendy Craig finds that this encompasses all that she holds dear, "God's precious and beautiful gifts which continue to inspire my life and work as I move forward into the unknown."

God of the Open Air

These are the things I prize
And hold of dearest worth:
Light of the sapphire skies,
Peace of the silent hills,
Shelter of forests, comfort of the grass,
Music of birds, murmur of little rills,
Shadows of cloud that swiftly pass,
And, after showers,
The smell of flowers
And of the good, brown earth –
And best of all, along the way, friendship and mirth.
So let me keep
These treasures of the humble heart
In true possession, owning them by love;
And when at last I can no longer move
Among them freely, but must part
From the green fields and waters clear,
Let me not creep
Into some darkened room and hide
From all that makes the world so bright and clear;
But throw the windows wide
To welcome in the light;
And while I clasp a well-beloved hand,
Let me once more have sight
Of the deep sky and the far-smiling land –
Then gently fall on sleep,
And breathe my body back to Nature's care,
My spirit out to thee, God of the open air.

Henry van Dyke

Peter Goringe, Deputy Director of Education (Schools), Diocese of Peterborough has chosen this verse from Ecclesiastes. Peter says that this is perhaps a strange choice for an educationalist, but a reminder that the Biblical writers knew that getting the right balance in our life is so important.

"My son, there is something else to watch out for. There is no end to the writing of books, and too much study will wear you out."

Ecclesiastes chapter 12, verse 12, Good News Bible.

Wendy Craig says that, "Despite the changes in society God never changes. His love and guidance are as reliable today as they ever were. He is the same yesterday, today and for ever. What a comfort!"

God is unchanging

Let nothing disturb you, nothing alarm you:
While all things fade away
God is unchanging.
Be patient
And you will gain everything:
For with God in your heart
Nothing is lacking,
God meets your every need.

St Teresa of Avila
(modern version by Henry Wadsworth Longfellow)

Chosen by Wendy Craig but a message for us all ……………

IF A CHILD ……

If a child lives with criticism,
she learns to condemn.
If a child lives with hostility,
she learns to fight.
If a child lives with ridicule,
she learns to be shy.
If a child lives with shame,
she learns to feel guilty.
If a child lives with tolerance,
she learns to be patient.
If a child lives with encouragement,
she learns confidence.
If a child lives with praise,
she learns to appreciate.
If a child lives with fairness,
she learns justice.
If a child lives with security,
she learns to have faith.
If a child lives with approval,
she learns to like herself.
If a child lives with acceptance and friendship,
she learns to find love in the world.

Author unknown

Wendy Craig had a strong faith from an early age but her fame and demands of show business led her away from God. Then, later in life, an emptiness and loneliness led her to a spiritual experience that took her back to her faith.
Wendy Craig has starred in many TV classics including, 'Not in Front of the Children' and 'Butterflies'. She has also appeared in many other television and stage dramas.

SHOW ME THE WAY

When I'm confused, Lord, show me the way
Show me, show me, the way
Baffled and bruised, Lord, show me the way
Show me, show me, show me the way

Still my heart and clear my mind
Prepare my soul to hear
Your still, small voice
Your word of truth
Peace be still your Lord is here.
Always so close to show you the way
Show you, show you, show you the way

When I'm afraid, Lord
Show me the way
Show me, show me, show me the way
Weak and dismayed, Lord
Show me the way
Show me, show me, show me the way

Lift my spirit with your love
Bring courage, calm and peace
You who bore all for my sake
So I could walk from fear released
With you beside me
Showing the way
Showing, showing, showing the way.

Wendy Craig

I wrote this song whilst walking in the countryside with my dog. I was asking God for guidance and as I was praying I began to sing. My sons' Ross and Alaster helped transcribe the words into song. It's a simple request to God to show me the way.

Sir Tim Smit KBE is famous for his work on the 'Lost Gardens of Heligan' and the 'Eden Project' both in Cornwall. Sir Tim continues to be the Chief Executive for the Eden Project.

Tim writes, "The poem that I always keep for inspiration is Sir Thomas Grey's 'Elegy Written in an English Country Churchyard' reflecting on the unrealised potential, yet latent talent of those buried there. For me, it has always been a call to arms, and as I have grown older it has become more and more apt as I realised that those who I would have looked up to when young, whether they be politicians, captains of industry or cultural icons, are, by and large, no more special than those of us of a more ordinary cut. If I had known that most of them are no different to us at that age, I would have set the bar of my aspirations far higher."

Elegy Written in an English Country Churchyard

**The Curfew tolls the knell of parting day,
The lowing herd wind slowly o'er the lea,
The plowman homeward plods his weary way,
And leaves the world to darkness and to me.**

**Now fades the glimmering landscape on the sight,
And all the air a solemn stillness holds,
Save where the beetle wheels his droning flight,
And drowsy tinklings lull the distant folds.**

**Save that from yonder ivy-mantled tow'r
The moping owl does to the moon complain
Of such as, wand'ring near her secret bow'r,
Molest her ancient solitary reign.**

**Beneath those rugged elms, that yew-tree's shade,
Where heaves the turf in many a mould'ring heap,
Each in his narrow cell for ever laid,
The rude Forefathers of the hamlet sleep.**

The breezy call of incense-breathing Morn,
The swallow twitt'ring from the straw-built shed,
The cock's shrill clarion, or the echoing horn,
No more shall rouse them from their lowly bed.

For them no more the blazing hearth shall burn,
Or busy housewife ply her evening care;
No children run to lisp their sire's return,
Or climb his knees the envied kiss to share.

Oft did the harvest to their sickle yield,
Their furrow oft the stubborn glebe has broke:
How jocund did they drive their team afield!
How bow'd the woods beneath their sturdy stroke!

Let not Ambition mock their useful toil,
Their homely joys, and destiny obscure;
Nor Grandeur hear with a disdainful smile
The short and simple annals of the poor.

The boast of heraldry, the pomp of pow'r,
And all that beauty, all that wealth e'er gave,
Awaits alike th' inevitable hour:
The paths of glory lead but to the grave.

Nor you, ye Proud, impute to These the fault,
If Memory o'er their Tomb no Trophies raise,
Where through the long-drawn aisle and fretted vault
The pealing anthem swells the note of praise.

Can storied urn or animated bust
Back to it's mansion call the fleeting breath?
Can Honour's voice provoke the silent dust,
Or Flatt'ry soothe the dull cold ear of death?

Perhaps in this neglected spot is laid
Some heart once pregnant with celestial fire;
Hands, that the rod of empire might have sway'd,
Or waked to ecstasy the living lyre.

But Knowledge to their eyes her ample page
Rich with the spoils of time did ne'er unroll;
Chill Penury repress'd their noble rage,
And froze the genial current of the soul.

Full many a gem of purest ray serene
The dark unfathom'd caves of ocean bear:
Full many a flower is born to blush unseen,
And waste its sweetness on the desert air.

Some village Hampden that with dauntless breast
The little tyrant of his fields withstood,
Some mute inglorious Milton here may rest,
Some Cromwell guiltless of his country's blood.

Th' applause of list'ning senates to command,
The threats of pain and ruin to despise,
To scatter plenty o'er a smiling land,
And read their history in a nation's eyes.

Their lot forbade: nor circumscribed alone
Their glowing virtues, but their crimes confined;
Forbade to wade through slaughter to a throne,
And shut the gates of mercy on mankind.

The struggling pangs of conscious truth to hide,
To quench the blushes of ingenuous shame,
Or heap the shrine of Luxury and Pride
With incense kindled at the Muse's flame.

Far from the madding crowd's ignoble strife,
Their sober wishes never learn'd to stray;
Along the cool sequester'd vale of life
They kept the noiseless tenor of their way.

Yet ev'n these bones from insult to protect
Some frail memorial still erected nigh,
With uncouth rhymes and shapeless sculpture deck'd,
Implores the passing tribute of a sigh.

Their name, their years, spelt by th' unletter'd muse,
The place of fame and elegy supply;
And many a holy text around she strews,
That teach the rustic moralist to die.

For who, to dumb Forgetfulness a prey,
This pleasing anxious being e'er resign'd,
Left the warm precincts of the cheerful day,
Nor cast one longing ling'ring look behind?

On some fond breast the parting soul relies,
Some pious drops the closing eye requires;
Ev'n from the tomb the voice of Nature cries,
Ev'n in our Ashes live their wonted Fires.

For thee, who, mindful of th' unhonour'd dead,
Dost in these lines their artless tale relate;
If chance, by lonely contemplation led,
Some kindred spirit shall inquire thy fate,

Haply some hoary-headed Swain may say,
'Oft have we seen him at the peep of dawn
Brushing with hasty steps the dews away
To meet the sun upon the upland lawn.

There at the foot of yonder nodding beech,
That wreathes its old fantastic roots so high,
His listless length at noontide would he stretch,
And pore upon the brook that babbles by.

Hard by yon wood, now smiling as in scorn,
Mutt'ring his wayward fancies he would rove,
Now drooping, woeful wan, like one forlorn,
Or crazed with care, or cross'd in hopeless love.

One morn I miss'd him on the custom'd hill,
Along the heath and near his fav'rite tree;
Another came; nor yet beside the rill,
Nor up the lawn, nor at the wood was he;

'The next with dirges due in sad array
Slow through the church-way path we saw him borne.
Approach and read (for thou canst read) the lay
Graved on the stone beneath yon aged thorn:'

The Epitaph

Here rests his head upon the lap of Earth
A Youth to Fortune and to Fame unknown.
Fair Science frown'd not on his humble birth,
And Melancholy mark'd him for her own.

Large was his bounty, and his soul sincere,
Heav'n did a recompense as largely send:
He gave to Mis'ry all he had, a tear,
He gain'd from Heav'n ('twas all he wish'd) a friend.

No farther seek his merits to disclose,
Or draw his frailties from their dread abode,
(There they alike in trembling hope repose,)
The bosom of his Father and his God.

The Right Honourable Michael Gove MP and Secretary of State for the Department of Education has chosen some favourite lines from John Donne's (1572-1631) prose. John was born into a Roman Catholic family when the general feeling in England was anti-catholic. After a turbulent life he took religious orders in 1615 and became Dean of St Paul's Cathedral in 1621. His private devotions and sacred writings were all published. 'For Whom the Bell Tolls' is a very famous piece of writing part of which is shown below..

FOR WHOM THE BELL TOLLS

"……….. No man is an island, entire of itself; every man is a piece of the continent, a part of the main. If a clod be washed away by the sea, Europe is the less, as well as if a promontory were, as well as if a manor of thy friend's or of thine own were; any man's death diminishes me, because I am involved in mankind, and therefore never send to know for whom the bell tolls; it tolls for thee …….. and so secure myself, by making my recourse to my God, who is our only security,"

Selected by Melanie Reid and it is a quote from Sir Sydney Smith (1771-1845). Melanie says that, "basically it underscores the most important message of all (as I have discovered): do not waste your life worrying or moaning or procrastinating, get out and live, enjoy the moment."

**"One great remedy is to take short views of life.
Are you happy now?
Are you likely to remain so till this evening?
Or next week?
Or next month?
Then why destroy present happiness with distant misery, which may never come at all, or you may never live to see?
For every substantial grief has twenty shadows, and most of them shadows of your own making."**

Melanie Reid is a journalist and an award winning columnist for The Times. In April 2010 Melanie fell off her horse. She broke her neck and back when the horse refused to jump a fence. Melanie is now tetraplegic and paralysed from the neck down. She has fought the disability to walk with aids, drive a car and even ride on a horse again. Melanie continues to write a weekly account in The Times Magazine about her successes and frustrations in overcoming her accident and subsequent disabilities.

Mike Ovey, Principal of Oak Hill College, London, has chosen his favourite prayer, the General Thanksgiving from the Book of Common Prayer, which has meant, "a good deal to me over the years."

Almighty God, father of all mercies, we, thine unworthy servants, do give thee most humble and hearty thanks for all thy goodness and loving-kindness to us and to all men. We bless thee for our creation, preservation, and all the blessings of this life; but above all, for thine inestimable love in the redemption of the world by our Lord Jesus Christ; for the means of grace, and for the hope of glory. And, we beseech thee, give us that due sense of all thy mercies, that our hearts may be unfeignedly thankful; and that we show forth thy praise, not only with our lips, but in our lives, by giving up ourselves to thy service, and by walking before thee in holiness and righteousness all our days; through Jesus Christ our Lord, to whom, with thee and the Holy Ghost, be all honour and glory, world without end. Amen.

Christine Burnett has worked in churches and schools and is currently School Support Officer at Bouverie Court, Northampton. This is a prayer she returns to time and time again.

> You are unique,
> You are beautiful,
> You are made in God's image,
> There is no one like you.
>
> You are special, you are once-only,
> You are never to be repeated,
> You ARE incredible.

Prayer by Mark Townsend and to be read in company with Psalm 139 verses 13-16.

Dear God,
I am sorry for the things I have done wrong, for my wrong thoughts, and for living without you. I believe Jesus died on the cross for me and took away my sins. I believe that He rose again from the dead. Please forgive me, take control of my life and, with the help of Your Holy Spirit, give me strength to live with you every day.
In the Name of Jesus,
Amen

This prayer written by Dorothy Carswell is found in her book 'Live Wires: Powerful Stories of Changed Lives' and published by 10Publishing.
Copyright © 2010 DJ Carswell
www.10ofthose.com

PARENTS, STAFF, GOVERNORS, PUPILS AND FRIENDS.

Beth

Invictus

Out of the night that covers me,
Black as the pit from pole to pole,
I thank whatever gods may be
For my unconquerable soul.

In the fell clutch of circumstance
I have not winced nor cried aloud.
Under the bludgeonings of chance
My head is bloody, but unbowed.

Beyond this place of wrath and tears
Looms but the Horror of the shade,
And yet the menace of the years
Finds and shall find me unafraid.

It matters not how strait the gate,
How charged with punishments the scroll,
I am the master of my fate:
I am the captain of my soul.

Chosen by Pete Holloway, parent and Foundation Governor.

This Victorian poem was written by the English poet William Ernest Henley in 1875 and was used by Nelson Mandela whilst he was imprisoned on Robben Island. Nelson Mandela would recite this poem to other prisoners and was empowered by its message of self-mastery. The poem has been used in a variety of films including Invictus, in which Nelson Mandela gives the captain of the national South African rugby team the poem to inspire him to lead his team to victory in the Rugby World Cup of 1995, telling him how it inspired him in prison.

If I speak in the tongues of men or of angels, but do not have love, I am only a resounding gong or a changing cymbal. If I have the gift of prophecy and can fathom all mysteries and all knowledge, and if I have a faith that can move mountains, but do not have love, I am nothing. If I give all I possess to the poor and give over my body to hardship that I may boast, but do not have love, I gain nothing.

Love is patient, love is kind. It does not envy, it does not boast, it is not proud. It does not dishonour others, it is not self-seeking, it is not easily angered, it keeps no record of wrongs. Love does not delight in evil but rejoices with the truth. It always protects, always trusts, always hopes, always perseveres.

Love never fails. But where there are prophecies, they will cease; where there are tongues, they will be stilled; where there is knowledge, it will pass away. For we know in part and we prophesy in part, but when completeness comes, what is in part disappears. When I was a child, I talked like a child; I thought like a child, I reasoned like a child. When I became a man, I put the ways of childhood behind me. For now we see only a reflection, as in a mirror; then we shall see face to face. Now I know in part; then I shall know fully, even as I am fully known.
And now these three remain: faith, hope and love. But the greatest of these is love.

1 Corinthians 13

This is our favourite reading from the Bible as it is so beautiful and full of hope. It is a lesson for everyone. We chose this simple translation as it is very easy for children to understand.

Chosen by *Daniel and Alice Rock*, parents.

Dear Father

Thank you for always being there for me. Thank you for giving me a home and family and freinds. Thank you for giving me peace and joy in the darkest hours.
You can always keep me on the right path, even if I might do something wrong. If there was one thing that would definatly come true, I'd wish for world peace, but for now please could you keep all less fortunate people safe and help those people who are very sick. Help me to be a better christian and to help others. Please help me to get along with other people and to keep me and every one happy. Please help me to persevere and never give up.
In Jesus christ our Lord.
Amen

Rebekah

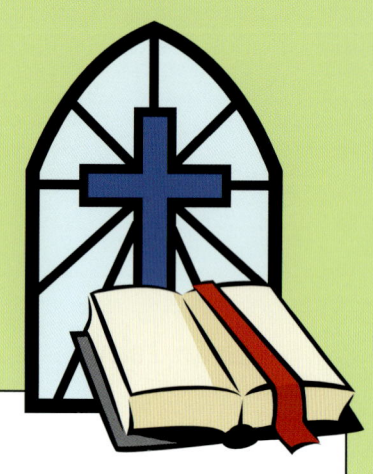

Thank you God for making everything and thank you God for making me.

A spontaneous prayer at bedtime,
Finlay (Kingdom Kids Church Group)

**Dear God,
Please can you protect me, my family, my friends and everyone else. Keep us safe wherever we are and whatever we are doing.
Amen**

Marcus (Kingdom Kids Church Group)

**Help us to do the things we should
To be to others kind and good
And in all we do and all we say
To grow more loving everyday.
Amen**

Felicity (Kingdom Kids Church Group)

Dear Lord,
Thank you for my school, my friends, everyone in the world and everything in the universe. Please help the people who do not have homes or a family.
Amen

Marcus

Dear God,
Thank you for the gift of life.
Thank you for friends and family.
Help the poor and the ill to be healthy and fit.
Keep them believing in You.
Amen

Josh

Bradley

Dear Lord,
Please help the people who are poorly and the people who are fighting for us. Please make sure that the people who are having a bad time have a good time.
Amen

Leon

Dear Lord,
Help the people who are fighting for us and please help the people in Africa who do not have much money or houses to live in. Please help them to have food.
Amen

Bryson

Dear Lord,
Help the poor people and the starving children in Africa and around the world. Help the people who are in Afghanistan. Thank you for my house and my family and friends.
Amen

Sam

Dear God,
Thank you for my food that is on my plate.
Thank you for all the animals and please help the sick animals.
I appreciate the men who fight in wars and the doctors who help the injured.
I am truly grateful to You for making me, my family and friends.
Amen

Zach

Dear Father,
Thank you for plants and people.
Please help people in different countries to survive.
Thank you for parents and police.
Help people who have cancer to survive.
Amen

Kacey

Oh Lord, help Patrick and Alex. Help them to be good firemen. Thank you for the world.
Amen

Joe

Dear God,
Thank you for my Mum and Dad for helping me make models and for cooking and loving me and taking me out. Thank you for my adorable sister Emily.
Amen

Thomas

Dear Lord,
Thank you for my friends and family.
Thank you for the world.
Please help the animals and plants to be healthy and to survive.
Help me to be a better person.
Amen

Alicia

Dear Lord,
Thank you for schools, teachers and my Mum and Dad. Help people who are starving and give them food and water. Thank you for my guinea pig called Twitch. I appreciate your love and affection.
Amen

Harry

Dear Lord
Thank you for my family and friends. Thank you for pets that keep us company. Thank you for our schools where we can learn. Thank you for our food and drink.
Amen

Bradley

Dear Father in Heaven,
Help the children in Africa, they are poor and have little food and drink. Give them faith and hope and I just want you to lay your hands on them and to say, 'do not worry, God is here.'
Amen

Katie

Dear God,
Thank you for the world, the birds, flowers and the animals. Thank you for my Mum and Dad and my house.
Amen

Lewis

Dear Lord,
Thank you for food and drink. Thank you for the animals living in the wild and the ones that are our pets. Thank you for my family and my friends.
Amen

Reece

Dear Lord,
Thank you for my Mum and Dad, who everyday do the cleaning, cooking and washing. Thank you that they give me cuddles and kisses and look after me. Thank you for my lovely Nan who helps me with stuff.
Amen

Chayden

Dear Lord,
Thank you for families and friends. You saved the world so I am going to thank you. I love everyone.
Amen

Tiana

Father God,
Please help people in faraway countries make peace and calmness.
Thank you for food, animals and for families and friends. The world is wonderful.
Amen

Charlotte

Katherine

Dear Lord,
Thank you for all the lovely food and water you give us. Thank you for our friends and family. Please can you help people who do not have a home to find one and pray for the people who fight for us. Thank you for our world and ourselves. I thank you for all the nice animals and help the animals that are sick.
Amen

Georgia

Do not fear, for I have redeemed you
I have called you by name, you are mine
When you pass through the waters, I will be with you;
And when you pass through the rivers,
They shall not overwhelm you …
Do not fear, for I am with you.

Selected by Elizabeth Brown, grandparent to Jessica.

Father,
Please help people in need and look after the world when the going is tough. Please help people be better Christians. Please help people believe in you so that their lives get better.
Father please help the world.
Amen

Rachel

Lord,
Thank you for our wonderful world.
Thank you for all the animals and plants too.
Please help all the people who need operations and other things they may be scared of. Be with them all the way through things that they worry about and look after them while they face it.
Amen

Eleanor

Beth

Dear Father,
Thank you for our family and friends and all the things we have. Thank you for our brothers and sisters and for looking after us. Help us to help the people in need. Thank you for those who fight for us and thank you for our mums and dads.
Amen

Juanita

Dear Father,
Please can you give peace and happiness to all people.

Lewis

FOOTPRINTS IN THE SAND

One night I dreamed I was walking
along the beach with the Lord.
Many scenes from my life flashed
across the sky. In each scene I
noticed footprints in the sand.
Sometimes there were two sets of
footprints, other times there was one
only. This bothered me because I
noticed that during the low periods of
my life, when I was suffering from
anguish, sorrow or defeat,
I could see only one set of footprints,
So I said to the Lord.
"You promised me Lord,
that if I followed you, you would walk
with me always. But I have noticed
that during the most trying periods of
my life there has only been one set of
footprints in the sand.
Why, when I needed you most, have
You not been there for me?"
The Lord replied,
"The years when you have seen only
one set of footprints,
my child, is when I carried you."

Chosen by Jennifer Parnell, parent.
Jennifer says that, "This helps me during the stressful
times to know that I don't walk alone."

You are at the beginning,
A new chapter of your life is opening,
At present the pages are blank,
But give God the pen and
He will write on every
New page of your life.

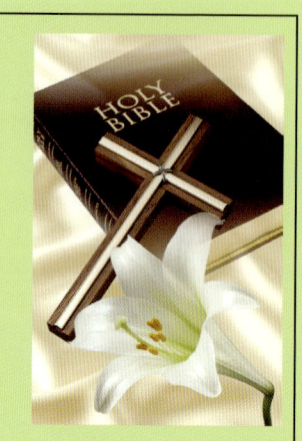

"I know the plans I have for you"
Jeremiah 29 v 11

Chosen by Libby Thomson, parent and Kingdom Kids Leader.

Dear God,
Thank you for the world.
Thank you for making us.
Thank you for the sun.
Thank you for the sky.
Thank you for my family.
Help people who are poorly.
Help people who are in hospital.
Help people who do not have a home.
Amen

Maddie

EDWARD

I can't write a poem about you
There's far too much to tell;
From your head to your toes
Well Heaven knows
You put together so well.

Just look at your hair
It's all curly.
And your eyes are wide and grey.
So I can't write a poem about you
There's far too much to say.

I would have to mention your lovely smile
And all the things you know;
You're a magical boy
And you fill me with joy
God knows I love you so.

When it's 3.15 on a weekday
It's CBeebies time;
We both watch TV
That's just you and me
I can't put all that into rhyme.

You're my wonderful beautiful grandson
A treasure in so many ways
So I can't write a poem about you
It would take me the rest of my days.

Written by Bettyne Bennett – a grandma to her grandson and chosen by Miles Bennett her son and Parent Governor.

LEISURE

What is this life if, full of care,
We have no time to stand and stare.

No time to stand beneath the boughs
And stare as long as sheep or cows.

No time to see, when woods we pass
Where squirrels hide their nuts in grass.

No time to see, in broad daylight,
Streams full of stars, like skies at night.

No time to turn at Beauty's glance,
And watch her feet, how they can dance.

No time to wait till her mouth can
Enrich that smile her eyes began.

A poor life this if, full of care,
We have no time to stand and stare.

William H Davies 1871-1940

Selected by Dr John Herrick, Chair of Sywell CEVA School Governors.

John says, "Modern life is hectic. I often turn to this poem to remind me to slow down and enjoy the world around me."

A WORD TO THE YOUNG

Please don't look at me with eyes that only see,
My wrinkled face and greying hair,
My ageing frame and slowing steps.
Please look at me and try to see
The person that I used to be.

I would run and dance and sing out loud.
My mind was sharp, I was the laughter maker in the crowd.
I dealt with problems in my life.
Reduced in being a mother and a wife.

So look kindly on me now when you come by my way.
And remember this, you will be me one day.

Bettyne Bennett, chosen by Miles Bennett, Parent Governor.

Dear Lord,
Please help all the English soldiers who are fighting in the war to protect our country. Help us to think about the people who are living in poverty. Thank you for the Queen's Diamond Jubilee. Help all the people in the world to practice and show perseverance for the 2012 Olympics.
Amen

Steven

Dear God,
Thank you for our friends and family. Please forgive us for the things that we have done that are wrong and help us to do better.
Amen

Hattie

Dear God,
Thank you for food and help the people who need food. Be with them when they are sad and hungry. Please help us and we know that you are special.
Amen

Maddison

Dear Lord,
Thank you for the world and our families. Thank you for God and Jesus and for the Holy Spirit. Thank you for this wonderful life.
Amen

Hannah

Dear God,
Thank you for our lovely world and the sun that shines on us. Thank you for homes and for everything that you have given us.
Amen

Louis

ALL I REALLY NEED TO KNOW I LEARNED IN KINDERGARTEN
A guide for Global Leadership

All I really need to know about how to live and what to do and how to be I learned in kindergarten. Wisdom was not at the top of the graduate school mountain, but there in the sand pile at school.

These are the things I learned.

Share everything.
Play fair.
Don't hit people.
Put things back where you found them.
Clean up your own mess.
Don't take things that aren't yours.
Say you're sorry when you hurt somebody.
Wash your hands before you eat. Flush.
Warm cookies and cold milk are good for you.
Live a balanced life – learn some and think some and draw and paint and sing and dance and play and work every day some.
Take a nap every afternoon.
When you go out in the world, watch out for traffic, hold hands and stick together.
Be aware of wonder.
Remember the little seed in the plastic cup, the roots go down and the plant goes up and nobody really knows how or why, but we are all like that.
Goldfish and hamsters and white mice and even the little seed in the plastic cup, they all die. So do we.
And then remember the Dick-and-Jane books and the first word you learned – the biggest word of all
LOOK
Everything you need to know is there somewhere.
Think of what a better world it would be if we all – the whole world shares everything.
Say sorry when you hurt others and when you just had to tell the truth.

And it is still true, no matter how old you are, when the going gets tough, it is best to hold hands and stick together.

This prose by Robert Fulgham has been Selected by Sue Gardner, Headteacher, Sywell CEVA Primary School.

God most high,

Please teach people in crime to understand how life could be. And show them that there should be no need for violence or verbal violence. Let there be consequences to our actions. Show us that kindness should always be welcome to all of our hearts. Help us to remember the values you taught us. Please love souls.

      Amen

Ellie

Reception Class September 2012

Dear Jesus, Please give a friend to God because he's really sad. Amen.

Jaycob

Dear God, Thank you for Mummy tucking me up in my warm, cosy bed. Amen

Evie

Father, Thank you for keeping my Dad safe. Amen.

Toby

Dear God, Thank you for giving Mummy baby Dolly. Amen.

Fergus

Dear Jesus, Please look after Grandma. Thank you. Amen.

Aaron

Father, Thank you for the moon. Amen.

Morgan

Dear Jesus, Thank you for letting me come to school. Amen.

Andrew

Dear Jesus, Thank you for the zoo. Amen

Caden

Reception Class September 2012

Good Father, Thank you for my Dad. Amen

Alfie

Dear Jesus, Thank you for looking after Grandma. Amen

Billie

Dear God, Thank you for my yummy dinners. Amen.

Sophie-Grace

Jesus Christ, Thank you for my friend Aaron. Amen

Gabriel

Thank you God for my Mummy. I love my Mummy. Amen.

Nathan

Dear Lord, Thank you for my Mummy and Daddy. I love them. Amen.

Lottie

Father, Thank you for the food we eat. Amen

Grace

Dear Heavenly Father,
Thank you for all our friendships and our family.
Most importantly thank you for our friendship with God and Jesus.
Amen

Aoife

Dear God,
Thank you for all our families and our pets. We pray for the people in hospital and that they get better. I hope that our families and friends stay healthy.
Amen

Amy

Dear God,
Let the people enjoy the peace and nature. Help everyone to go safely to Heaven. I hope that there will be peace in the world.
Amen

James

Heavenly Father,
Thank you for the church.
Thank you for the people who help us.
Thank you for the world and flowers.
Thank you for fun.
Amen

Max

Dear God
Please can you stop people testing on animals who have not done anything wrong. Take care of all creatures and animals in this world.
Amen

Troy

To our Heavenly Father God,

People in this world are less fortunate than some. Others have a lot more than those less fortunate. They have a warm bed to sleep in. Some don't. They have enough food to last a long time. Some don't. They have a good job and a good amount of money. Some don't. They have a good school to go to. Some don't. Please help those who are in need, those who suffer, and those who are fighting to help our country. Also, please send a blessing all around the world. Into every soul, every sin. All of those who have made mistakes in life, please forgive them.

Amen

Roisin

Dear God,
Please let our family and friends have a good life and help them to be the best they can. Make them have lots of fruits and vegetables.
Amen

Holly

Dear our Heavenly Father,

In our world it's a shame to watch people get ill, for the people who have diseases please help them to feel better. May the companionship in the world grow stronger every day and for those who are upset to feel happier. Help people in poverty Lord, help them live in peace. Lord help our world become a better place.

Amen

Emily

Dear God,
Thank you for the food and help the other people in need. Please help the poor to have water.
Amen

Taylor

Dear Heavenly Father,
Help every person in need to get well. Help raise money to save those people. Help people to have fun. Jesus died for us.
Amen

Bradley

Dear Lord,
Thank you for everything that you have given us in this world. Help other people in different countries. Thank you for our world. Thank you God for being with me.
Amen

Caitlin

Dear God,
Thank you for the lovely food and drink. Thank you for my lovely family.
Amen

Kian

Dear Lord,
Thank you for family and friends and for food and water. Please help the people who are hungry and thirsty, please give them clean water to drink and make their world a happier place. Thank you God for the flowers, the trees and the buzzy bees. Help me to persevere and carry on.
Amen

Alexandra

Dear Holy Lord,

Please help us to be kind, caring, loyal to others, happy, detirmind but most of all compassionate. We know how to act but we don't usually remember. Next time when we're about to do something wrong, please make us stop and think about it before we do so.
Thank you Lord that we can have different feelings and emotions for the rest of our lives.

Amen

Sarah

Trust him
when dark doubts attack you,
Trust him
when your strength is small,
Trust him
when to simply trust him
is the hardest thing of all.

Trust him
he is ever faithful,
Trust him
for his will is best.
Trust him
for the Heart of Jesus,
is the only place to rest.

Trust him
Then through doubts
and sunshine,
All your cares
upon him cast,
Till the storm of life
is over,
and your trusting days
are past.

Lisa Sims, Jennifer Parnell's sister selected this prose. She says, "It helped me a lot one time when everything was going wrong for me." Both Jennifer and Lisa are former pupils at Sywell CEVA School.

Dear Lord,
Thank you so much for creating the world. I am very grateful to you but please help the people in need of homes. Please talk to the robbers so that they change their ways. Thank you so much. Amen

Daisy

John Wesley the Founder of Methodism used this prayer, which is still used today, during the services as a Renewal of the believer's Covenant with God.

I am no longer my own, but thine.
Put me to what thou wilt, rank me with whom thou will.
Put me to doing, put me to suffering.
Let me be employed for thee or laid aside for thee,
exalted for thee or brought low for thee.
Let me be full, let me be empty.
Let me have all things, let me have nothing.
I freely and heartily yield all things to thy pleasure and disposal.
And now, O glorious and blessed God, Father, Son and Holy Spirit,
Thou art mine, and I am thine.
So be it.
And the covenant which I have made on earth, let it be ratified in heaven.
Amen

Selected by the Reverend Duncan Beet, Priest-in-Charge at Sywell, Overstone, Mears Ashby and Hardwick. Duncan is also a parent and Foundation Governor.

Dear Lord,
Please help the people who haven't got any food. Please help the world to be a better place so everyone has enough food and water. Make sure that people live in peace. Help the people who have diseases and are ill. Help people to realise that God is always there.
Amen

Ella-Jay

Dear Lord,

Please help when people are poorly and sick. Help the world when wrong things happen. Help all the children in need. Please look after my family and friends. Give people mercy and look down upon them. When people do wrong please forgive them.
Amen

Abbie

Dear Lord,
Help the soldiers at war to battle through their pain. Help the children moving through life and please help me persevere and not to give up. Make sure we do not feel blue. Thank you for our wonderful school and help us to learn lots.
Amen

Chris

Dear God,
Thank you for Jesus and the four seasons. We are thankful for your presence. Thank you for our families, friends and school.
Amen

Isabella

Dear Lord,
Help everyone who is starving at this moment and pray for everyone who does not have a home.
Thank you Lord for all I have and thank you that I can eat and drink every day. Help the people who are not very well and heal them with you special powers. Lord thank you for the world and every person, creature and plants. Our world is so beautiful. Thank you for being with everyone.
Amen

Simeon

Dear Father,
Please help people who are hungry and thirsty. Help these people who need a place to live and who need someone to take care of them and look after them. Help the people who are in need and less fortunate. Thank you for people who help others in many ways.
Amen

Sydney

Dear Father,
Thank you that you died on the cross for us. Thank you for the four seasons. Thank you that you love us.
Amen

Thomas

Dear Lord,
Everyone is thankful for what you do for us. We are all thankful for you creating us and for Adam and Eve. All of us are glad you created animals, trees and bushes. Everyone is happy that Jesus died on the cross for us.
Amen

Charlotte

Dear God,
We thank you for taking up your time to make this world and all the living creatures. Thank you for giving us eyes to see, ears to hear and hands to touch.
Amen

Charlie

Dear God,
Please help people who are sick and poor and have no family to look after them and to make them healthy. Please help orphans and people who live on the streets to find a home. God please help the people in need.
Amen

Caitlin

Heavenly Father,
Thank you for the world and the animals and for the jungles. We love all the animals from the tiny ant to the giant elephant. I love every single thing. Thank you.
Amen

Grace

Dear Lord,
Thank you for our families that help and care for us. That our school is one big family that tries to get along and help us to think about the people who help our school be a better place. Please Lord, help us think of all the people in the world who do not have a school of lovely people or a family to love and take care of them to help them learn.
Amen

Emily

Dear God,
Thank you for all the beautiful creations in the world. Thank for always being there for us and helping us through hard times.. Thank you for friends and family that look after us. Thank you for the lovely food you provide for us. Thank you for the lovely plants that give us oxygen that we breathe and thank you for people who help us.
Amen

Mayah

Dear Lord,
Help the poor and save us from diseases. Please help our family and friends. Heavenly Father, thank you for the lovely world and please make the world a better place to live.
Amen

Zak

Dear Lord. Thank you for family and friends. Thank you for the joy they bring me. They make me feel happy. Shine your love on them for looking after me when I'm ill and caring for me when I'm sad. Amen

Harry

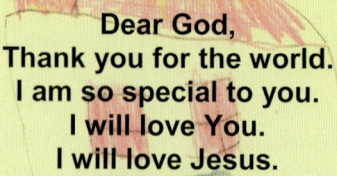

Dear God,
Thank you for the world.
I am so special to you.
I will love You.
I will love Jesus.
Help people who are sick and help people in need.
Amen

Jessica

Dear God,
Thank you for making the flowers and us. Thank you for the beautiful world and animals. Thank you for our friends and families. Thank you for friendship.
Amen

Lisa

Ella

Dear God,
Thank you for the gift of sight, smell, touch, taste and hearing. Please bless the people who are not so fortunate, those who do not possess the wonderful senses. Help us who do to treasure these gifts that you have created and to use them well.
Amen

Beth

A series of prayers written by the Reception Class in the summer of 2012

Father
Thank you for all the beautiful things in the world – like the flowers and the grass. I like the houses and the people in the houses.
Amen

Ella

Father
Thank you for my house, for my garden and my mummy's car.
Amen

Isla

Father
Thank you for the trains that I have. Thank you for my cuddly toys.
Amen

Finlay

Father
Thank you for all the things. Thank you for looking after us.
Amen

Jules

Father
Thank you for all the good things that have happened today, for fun with my friends.
Amen

Zara

Reception Class 2012

Dear God
Thank you for looking after us. I like you because you always love me.
Amen

Emily

Dear God
Thank you for all the children playing.
Amen

Freya

Dear God
Thank you for all the animals in the world. Thank you for the giraffes, hamsters, dogs and cats.
Amen

Emma

Father
Thank you God for everything like dance and football. I like listening to music. Thank you for Mummy and Daddy.
Amen

Poppy

Dear God
I love you because I like it when you pray with me. Thank you for helping me pray.
Amen

Jeremiah

Reception Class 2012

Dear God
I love you because you are nice. We cannot see you but I love you so much. You rescue us from evil.
Amen

Benjamin

Father
I love you. Thank you for the world – it's so sweet. I like playing with my birthday toys.
Amen

Ellie

Dear God
Thank you for my house and my family. Thank you for toys and friends. Help me mending stuff like my Dad.
Amen

Felix

Father,
Thank you for all the things that have happened today. Thank you for giving me my toys.
Amen

Grace

Dear God
Thank you for loving me. Thank you for letting me play with my friends. Thank you for my house and my family.
Amen

Zoe

Dear Lord God
   Thank you that you made the world for us
thankyou for the leaves, trees, stars and sky,
and the birds passing by.
For friends, family, a wonderful sight,
Lord you made the day and night.
You made our bodies so we could walk,
you made our mouthes so we could talk.
   Thank you God for the world it is oh so
sweet, you did well to give us that treat.

Amen

Hannah

Father,
Thank you for the wonderful music that we sing and dance to, it makes people feel happy and excited. Please keep music playing for ever and ever.
Amen

Joey

Holy Father,
Thank you for the world today and its magnificent beauty. Thank you for all the different cultures and countries and how you make them all so different. Help us to think about the different places - the mountains, forests and deserts.
Bless our world and its different places O Lord.
Amen

Abi

Dear Father,
Thank you for my family and my friends. Thank you for the people that help us. Firemen, police, doctors, and teachers at school.
Amen

Samuel

Father,
Please can you stop the floods because some people are losing their lives. Please help look after everyone and make sure they have a safe life.
Amen

Ross

Dear Lord

Help people who are injured or sick. Bless the people who help them and make sure that they are able to go on. If they are not able to go on help them or leave them be. Try to teach the people who are greedy and have a thirst for money to give and not keep. Thanks be to God

Amen

Megan

Dear Lord
Thank you for the school so that we can learn and get good jobs. Thank you for the seas and the wonderful trees that we all appreciate.
Thank you for the world that you made for us but sadly many people do not appreciate it.
The world will never be perfect, there will always be people who are not nice.
Please help to make the world a better place for us all.
Amen

Abbie

Dear God,
Please bless our wonderful world and all the people that live in it. Help us to think about other religions. We thank you that we know that we can pray to you anywhere, in a Mandir, in a church or even at home when we are with our family. Help us to remember that your Son was for all of us. The time of the year is close as we remember how the three kings travelled down to Bethlehem and gave their gifts – gold, frankincense and myrrh.
Amen

Seanna

Lord,
Please may there be no war or fighting. May everyone get along with each other. Please may the world live in peace and then we all will be happy.
Amen
Georgina

LIGHT OF THE WORLD

You are the Light of the World,
A city on a hill cannot be hidden,
Neither do people light a lamp
and put it under a bowl,
Instead they put it in a stand
and it gives light to everyone in the house.
(*At this point a candle can be lit*)
O God, grant me light in my heart
And light in my tongue.
Light in my hearing
And light in my seeing.
Light in my flesh, light in my blood,
Light in my bones.
Light before me, light behind me,
Light to the right of me,
Light to the left of me,
Light above me, light beneath me.
O God increase my light
And grant me to know the greatest light of all
Jesus Christ Our Lord.

Chosen by Tony Noble, Grandparent and Foundation Governor.
"I like to think of this prayer as God's Light shining down throughout the world. It makes me feel part of the whole world wide Christian community."

This prayer together with the lighting of a candle is often used in church services.

Dear Lord,
Please help the people in war and help the people in poverty. Thank you for the trees, bees, mountains and the animals and your Son Jesus Christ.
Amen

Edward

Bailey

Dear Lord

Thank you for the world and all of the animals. Lord you are the one! you are the one who made the world. Thank you for my friends and family Amen

Dear Lord,
Thank you for the lovely food you give everybody everyday.
Thank you for making this beautiful world.
Amen

Thomas

Father,
Thank you for the bees that buzz around the trees.
Thank you for the fish that swim about in the sea.
Thank you for the birds that fly about in the sky.
Thank you for the apes that swing about in the trees.
Thank you for the wonderful world we live in.
Amen

Myles

Dear God,
Thank you for all our friends, boys and girls.
They are all great.
For our friendships. They help us when we are hurt. They play with us when we are sad.
In the name of Jesus.
Amen

William

Dear Lord,
Thank you for the wonderful world you gave us my Lord.
Please protect our friends and teachers.
Please protect our school and parents.
Amen

Edmack

Desiderata

Go placidly amid the noise and the haste, and remember what peace there may be in silence. As far as possible without surrender be on good terms with all persons.

Speak your truth quietly, clearly; and listen to others, even to the dull and the ignorant, they too have their story. Avoid loud and aggressive persons, they are vexations to the spirit.

If you compare yourself to others, you may become vain and bitter; for always there will be greater and lesser persons than yourself.

Enjoy your achievements as well as your plans. Keep interested in your own career, however humble; it is a real possession in the changing fortunes of time.

Exercise caution in your business affairs, for the world is full of trickery. But let not this blind you to what virtue there is; many persons strive for high ideals, and everywhere life is full of heroism.

Be yourself. Especially do not feign affection. Neither be cynical about love; for in the face of all aridity and disenchantment it is as perennial as the grass. Take kindly the counsel of the years, gracefully surrendering the things of youth.

Nurture strength of spirit to shield you in sudden misfortune. But do not distress yourself with dark imaginings. Many fears are born of fatigue and loneliness.

Beyond a wholesome discipline, be gentle with yourself. You are a child of the universe, no less than the trees and the stars; you have a right to be here. And whether or not it is clear to you, no doubt the universe is unfolding as it should.

Therefore, be at peace with God, whatever you conceive him to be, and whatever your labours and aspirations in the noisy confusion of life, keep peace in your soul. With all it's sham drudgery and broken dreams; it is still a beautiful world.

Be cheerful. Strive to be happy.

Chosen by Cathy Woodruff, parent and Associate Governor.

Dear God,
Thank you for our world and that we are lucky enough to have our brilliant family and friends. Thank you for all our wonderful things you have given us. I am so special to you. The world is wonderful because you made it, all the plants, trees, the bees for nectar and the food and water to help us live. Thank you Lord.
Amen

Layla

Dear Holy Father,
Please help us to make the world a better place and let us think how the world could be. Help the people in Afghanistan and make the war end soon. Please help people to stay well and not get diseases. Help the people who are homeless and less fortunate than us. Bless the world.
Amen

Edward

Dear Lord,
Please help people who are attacking others and especially the people who are destroying people's homes. Please try to help people in the war areas, the casualties and dying. Please tell the British and Afghanistan people to get along together. Please make all wars to stop. Please help the police who try to stop the killing. Please help make the world a better place.
For Jesus Christ.
Amen

Sam

Dear Father
Please can you give peace and happiness to all people. There are lots of people out there in the world who have a serious condition or people who are ill. Please help them. Thank you for the charities that help the people and families in need of clothes, food and shelter.
Amen

Lewis

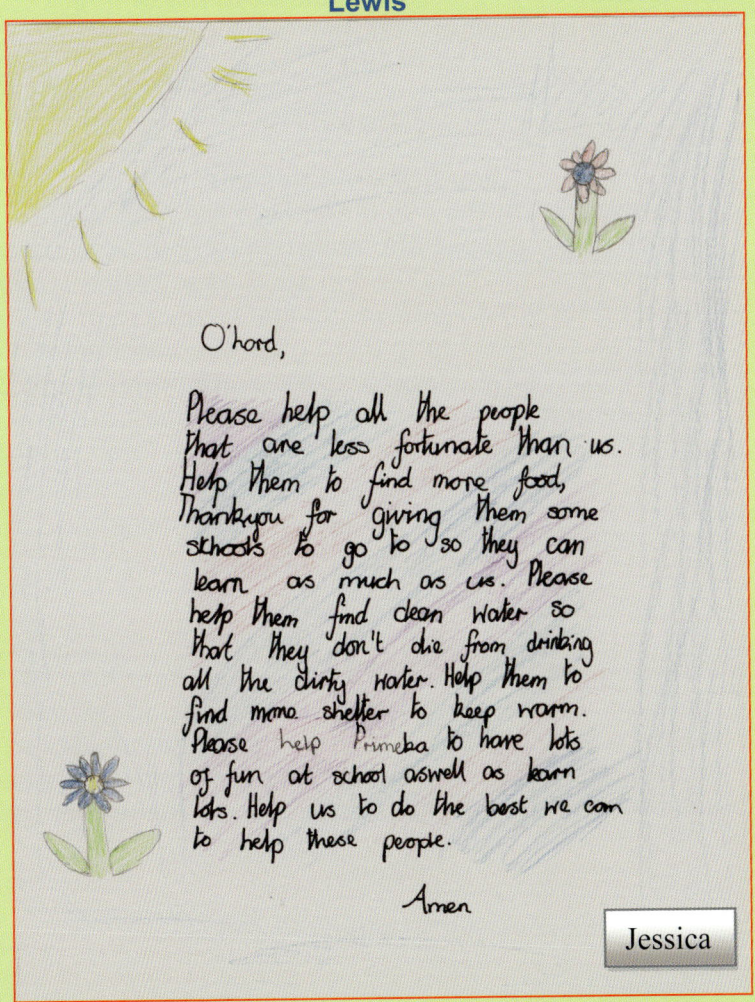

O'hord,

Please help all the people that are less fortunate than us. Help them to find more food, Thankyou for giving them some schools to go to so they can learn as much as us. Please help them find clean water so that they don't die from drinking all the dirty water. Help them to find more shelter to keep warm. Please help Primeba to have lots of fun at school aswell as learn lots. Help us to do the best we can to help these people.

Amen

Jessica

Dear Christ Our Lord,
Thank you for making the world a loving and caring place for people who are in need and let the people with problems who do not have much money or food to have peace in their lives.
Please do not let people suffer in big or small problems – let them stay calm.
Amen

Charlotte

Dear Father in Heaven,
Thank you for the world and everybody in it, but please help people who are in poverty or who are homeless and have no food at all. Please help us to be grateful for what we have got and to give to others with grace. Please help us to grow kind and helpful towards God. Please help us think about the people who are going through a hard time, like people who are fighting in the wars, or the families of soldiers who have died in the wars.
Amen

Alex

God most high,
Please teach people in crime to understand how life could be. Please show them that there is no need for violence verbal abuse. Let there be consequences to our actions. Show us that kindness should always be welcome to all of our hearts. Help us to remember the values you taught us.
Amen

Ellie

Dear Lord,
Thank you for your amazing creation and help us to remember it. We pray for less fortunate people than us that you will keep them safe. Help us to prepare for big events ahead but still keep faith in you.
Help us to make the world a better place by living in a manner that will help the world in many ways. So help us to remember you when I see some of the unexplainable sights of your creation.
In Jesus name.
Amen

Joel

MAASAI TRIBAL SAYINGS

"I believe in the spirit of sharing and I believe we are what we are because of those around us."
"I am what I am because of other people and they are what they are because of me being around."
"One hand cannot clap on its own but it needs the other hand to make it clap."
"Many hands make light work."

Selected by Steve Morrow, parent and Foundation Governor.

A VOLUNTEER'S PRAYER

I thank Thee, Lord as a volunteer
For the chance to serve another year.
And to give of myself in some small way,
To those not blessed as I each day.

My thanks for health and mind and soul,
To aid me ever toward my goal.
For eyes to see the good in all,
A hand to extend before a fall.
For legs to go where the need is great,
Learning to love – forgetting hate.
For ears to hear and heart to care,
When someone's cross is hard to bear.
A smile to show my affection true,
With energy aplenty - the task to do.

And all I ask, dear Lord, if I may,
Is to serve you better day by day.

Selected by Steve Morrow, parent and Foundation Governor.

"I have been a volunteer Police Officer for twenty years and feel that this prayer is appropriate for all who volunteer."

POLICEMAN'S PRAYER

Saint Michael, Heaven's glorious commissioner of police, who once so neatly and successfully cleared God's premises of all its undesirables, look with kindly and professional eyes on your earthly force.
Give us cool heads, stout hearts, and uncanny flair for investigation and wise judgement.
Make us the terror of burglars, the friend of children and law-abiding citizens, kind to strangers, polite to bores, strict with law-breakers and impervious to temptations.
You know, Saint Michael, from your own experiences with the devil, that the police officer's lot on earth is not always a happy one, but your sense of duty that so pleased God, your hard knocks that so surprised the devil, and your angelic self-control give us inspiration.
And when we lay down our night sticks, enrol us in your heavenly force, where we will be as proud to guard the throne of God as we have been to guard the city of all people.
Amen.

Selected by Pete Holloway, parent and Foundation Governor.

END THOUGHTS

BEFORE YOU SPEAK

T--- is it true
H--- is it helpful
I---- is it inspiring
N--- is it necessary
K--- is it kind

Immediately on entering our home you will find this on the hall wall. A constant reminder.

Tony and Margaret Noble, grandparents.

There is so much good in the worst of us,
And so much bad in the best of us,
That it hardly becomes any of us,
To talk about the rest of us.

Anon

God pays debts without money.

Laugh and say nothing.

J O Y
Jesus first .... **Y**ourself last
Others in between

A DAILY PRAYER

May there always be
A star to guide you
A friend beside you
A smile to cheer you
Loved ones near you
A fire to warm you
A prayer to say ….
And joy as bright
As each new day.

Lisa Sims (page 100) says, "It's my greatest sin to think I can do it on my own and that it's all about me. I now have a wall plaque of Proverbs 3:6 and it gives me a daily reflection."

'In all your ways acknowledge Him, and He will direct your path'.

May the road rise to meet you.
May the wind be always at your back.
May the sun shine warm upon your face.
May the rains fall softly upon your fields.
Until we meet again,
May God hold you in the hollow of his hand.

Traditional Irish Blessing

God Knows

And I said to the man who stood at the gate:
"Give us light that I may tread safely into the unknown."

And he replied:

"Go out into the darkness and put your hand in the hand of God.
That shall be to you better than light and safer than a known way."

This poem written by Minnie L Haskins has been widely used over the 20th century. It was used by King George 6th to finish his Christmas radio broadcast on December 25th 1939 as the nation braced itself for World War II.

Whatever you are – be that,

Whatever you say – be true,

Straightforwardly act,

Be honest – in fact

Be nobody else but you.

Inscription found on an old vase.

May God bless us,
That in us may be found
love and humility,
obedience and thanksgiving,
discipline, gentleness and peace.